What School Should Have Taught You

What School Should Have Taught You

75 Skills You'll Actually Use in Life

Aden Tate

Banned Books Publishing

Cheyenne, Wyoming

What School Should Have Taught You Copyright © 2022 by Banned Books Publishing. All Rights Reserved.

Contents

Dedication	xi
Disclaimer	xii
Foreword	1

Cars

How to Change a Flat Tire	7
What to Do if Your Car Breaks Down in the Middle of Nowhere	11
How to Jump Start a Car	15
Basic Car Maintenance	17
What to Do if You Run Out of Gas	21
How to Shop for a Car	23

Money

How to Set Up a Bank Account (and why you should)	33
How to Maintain a Budget	38
What to Do With Debt	43
Understanding Compounding Interest	46

Why You Should Shop Around Before Making Big Purchases	49
How to Negotiate	51
Carry Cash	53
All About Credit Cards	55
How to Write a Check	58
How and When to Tip	62
Couponing	64
How to Save for Retirement	67
What is Your Credit Score?	70
How to Pay Bills	72
How to do Taxes	75
Writing a Will	80

Food

Kitchen Utensils That You Will Need	85
How to Shop for Groceries	87
Easy-to-Cook Meals	90

Health

How to Navigate Healthcare	95
Basic Medicines	97
Emergency Medical Situations	100
What to Do If You Get in a Car Accident	101
Why and How You Should Exercise	105
What to Do if You Get Pregnant	108

Safety

General Safety	113
What to Do if You Get Mugged	121
What are Your Rights When Interacting with Police	125
Self-Defense	127

Home

How to Shop for an Apartment	131
Basic Tools You Should Have	134
How to Clean a House	139
How to Patch a Hole in Drywall	143
How to Use a Plunger	144
How to Hang a Picture	146
What to Do with a Clogged Sink	149
Lawnmower stuff	151
Household Items You Will Need	153
How to Shop for Furniture	156
How to Do Laundry	159
How to Iron Clothes	162
I Want to Build Things with Tools but I Live in an Apartment!	164
What to Do If You Move	166
What to Do When the Power Goes Out	169

Life

All About Insurance	179
How to Small Talk Without Being Awkward	187
The Rules of Social Media	192
Basic Etiquette	197
Basic Dinner Etiquette	199
Tips on Buying an Engagement Ring	203
Random Relationship Tips	208
How to Plan a Wedding	216
How to Get a Passport	218
How to Tie a Tie	220
How to Vote	222
Where to Buy Stamps	225
Mailing Things Bigger than Letters	227

Job

How to Choose a Job You'd Be Happy With	233
How to Look for a Job	237
How to Write a Resume	242
Basic Interview Skills	244
Basic Job Skills	247
How to Open a Business	251

School

Looking at Continuing Your Education	257

How to Apply to College	261
How to Find Scholarships for College	266
Wrapping it Up	269
Further Reading	271
References	272

How to Apply to College	261
How to Find Scholarships for College	266
Wrapping it Up	269
Further Reading	271
References	272

Dedication

To my family. I love you fiercely.

Disclaimer

I am neither a lawyer, doctor, counselor, nor financial advisor. I do not pretend to be any of these things. None of this is medical, legal, or financial advice, and is only presented for information and entertainment purposes.

When I graduated from high school, I went straight to college. It seemed like the smart thing to do at the time. Getting an education was all but guaranteed to land me a six-figure job the day after I graduated. At least that's what I was led to believe. I quickly found out that unless you majored in petroleum engineering in college, the widely held belief that headhunters from multiple blue-chip corporations would come begging at your door for your application was simply a myth that your culture has told you.

What I also discovered was that school did NOT prepare me for real life.

All of those physics, calculus, and British lit classes may have helped you to keep your grades high enough to play for your high school football team (and yeah, they probably helped make you a more well-rounded person), but what they didn't do was prepare you for what the real world is like.

Up until you're in the "real" world, nothing will. Odds are if you're reading this, you've spent the past 18+ years living with your parents. That's a good thing, and they've undoubtedly taught you a myriad of great things about life. My parents did as well.

However, when you get out into the "real" world, when school is no longer taking up the majority of your day, you quickly realize that there is a lot going on out there that you need to know about that school did not teach you about.

Things like:

- how to shop for an apartment
- how to maintain a budget
- how to write a check
- how to do basic car maintenance
- and a host of other issues

Yes, your parents may have taught you how to do some of these things (and if they did you're incredibly blessed), but odds are there are still a few things out there that you have questions about.

That's what this book is for.

Real life for me was like a slap in the face. I quickly discovered that I was a veeeeeeery little fish in a big pond, and that unless I learned some fundamental life skills quick I was going to be a dirt poor slob living in a broken down refrigerator box. (Not even a *working* refrigerator box. A broken down one. I guess that means the cardboard has holes?)

The following pages are an accumulation of just some of the life skills that I had to learn along the way. Things that I had no idea what to do with, and that you may not as well. If that sounds like you, then welcome to the club. If you're flipping through this book right now and can't believe there are people out there that don't know this stuff, then that's cool as well. Just understand that you're blessed, and do what you can to help others around you who may need a little help just starting out learning what you now know.

For the rest of us, read on. I hope that you'll find not only encouragement but the practical know-how that school never taught you.

CARS

Unless one lives in a very congested urban environment where you can either walk, cycle, or take the subway everywhere, it is virtually impossible to survive without a car in modern-day America. Unfortunately, too many don't learn the basics of car ownership as they are growing up.

This lack of knowledge can not only prove to be dangerous, but expensive as well. Here is a collection of some of the more basic car owner tasks you wish school would have taught you.

How to Change a Flat Tire

I've had a flat tire or two, but my wife has had a flat tire or dozen. She somehow has wheels that magically attract every nail, screw, and pointy object from both lanes of the highway. As a result, I've gotten quite a bit of practice with replacing flat tires.

So if you ever find yourself stranded on the side of the road on the way to that important meeting (that's when these things happen, trust me), hopefully, this will give you the knowledge to get out of the situation as quickly as possible.

ALWAYS make sure that you have the car parked in an area where you are not going to get hit by other cars as you are changing the flat. If you can, see if you can pull your car into a gas station, parking lot, or another area where you are out of the way of incoming traffic. Also make sure that you are not stopped on an incline or on soft, squishy ground. Both of those are extremely important, but we'll come back to them later.

Turn the car off, and put the emergency brake on. You're going to be jacking your car up. Other than being hit by oncoming traffic, that last thing that you want to happen is for your car to start rolling while you have it jacked. So, pull the e-brake.

Most cars keep all the tools that you need to change

a flat tire in the trunk. The flooring of most trunks can actually be lifted up, and when it is you'll find all of the tools organized into a nice little pile. What you should see is: the jack, the tire iron, and the wheel.

If you do not see the wheel, it may actually be stored up underneath your car exposed to the road. These types of cars typically have an incredibly long bolt or cable that goes through the tire, through the bottom of the trunk, and then is secured from the inside of the trunk. If this is your type of car, you are going to first need to loosen whatever is keeping the tire snug against the car. Look around the inside of the trunk for something that you may need to twist.

Make sure that you have the car on solid, level ground. If you are on an incline and try to jack up your car, the car could fall off the jack and hurt you or seriously damage your car. If you are parked on unstable ground such as wet grass, gravel, mud, or the like, your car could fall off the jack and hurt you or seriously damage your car. Make sense?

Take your jack out and go to the flat tire. If the flat tire is a front tire, then you are going to place the jack on the car frame BEHIND that tire. If the flat tire is a rear tire, then you are going to place the jack on the car frame IN FRONT of that tire. Place the jack on the ground and start to raise it by twirling the lever. You want to ensure that the top of the jack touches the car frame, not the exterior frame. The car frame is the big bar of metal underneath the car roughly in-line with the middle of the side of the tires.

The car frame can support the pressure of the jack underneath of it. If the jack starts to put pressure anywhere else, that specific part of the car may not be able to hold the weight and it could be damaged and/or cause the car to fall off of the jack.

On a side note, NEVER place your head underneath a jacked-up car to have a little look-see as to what is going on under there. People have been decapitated that way when the car fell off of the jack and slammed through their vertebrae. You don't want that to be you.

Once the car is jacked up and all of the weight is off of the damaged tire, take the tire iron (the long bar with the wrench bit at one end, and take the nuts off of the damaged tire. You'll want to take the nuts off in a star pattern. You know how you can draw a 5-pointed star without lifting the pencil? That's the same basic pattern that you're going to follow to take the nuts off.

Otherwise, by taking the nuts off in a circular pattern you can cause the tire to go crooked, making it devilishly difficult to take it off when you need to. Also, make sure that you only loosen all of the nuts the first go-round through the star shape. This also helps to ensure that the tire doesn't get skewed on. After you have gone through the star pattern the first time and loosened all of the nuts, go back through the star pattern again to take all of the nuts off.

Now you're going to take the flat tire off. Pull it straight towards you. It's heavy, so be prepared.

Now put the spare tire (also referred to as a 'donut') on. It's going to look ridiculously puny compared to your normal tire, but that's ok. Place it on where the old tire once was, and make sure that you are placing it on facing the correct way. The spare should specifically say on it which side faces out.

After you have the spare tire on correctly, put the nuts back on the bolts again in the star pattern. You want to go through the star pattern the first go round and just make sure that the nuts are snug. The second go-round through the star pattern you're going to want to make sure that you have those bad boys on there tight. Nothing like having a wheel fall off while you're driving to keep you awake.

Throw the flat tire in the trunk as well as all of the tools, and you should be good to go until you can get your tire replaced. Be aware that you can't drive at the typical speed that you normally would with a donut. The spare on my car can only safely handle 55mph, so if you're on the interstate, drive in the right lane and drive what your spare says it can handle safely.

Also, you don't want to drive on these things forever. Try to get your new tire as quickly as you can. Don't drive on a donut for several days/weeks/hundreds of miles. The little thing can wear out pretty quickly if you do, and then you'll not only need to buy a new tire, you'll need to buy a new spare as well.

What to Do if Your Car Breaks Down in the Middle of Nowhere

Sooner or later your car *will* break down. It's not a matter of if, it's a matter of when. Unfortunately, that's just how it works, and if you ask just about anybody else around you they'll tell you that it is going to happen at the most inconvenient time possible.

Being stuck on the side of the road absolutely clueless isn't a fun place to be. There are some things that you can do though to get you the help you need.

Pull the car out of the road if possible – Having your car stuck at a dead stop in the middle of the road is a recipe for disaster. Not only could you get badly injured by an oncoming car, but that person in the oncoming car could get injured as well, and when other people get injured because of your car it can mean some legal nightmares.

Pull off onto the side if you can, and hit your hazard light switch. That way people will at least be aware that your car is having an issue. If your car decided to die while you were waiting for the light to change at that busy intersection, pulling over to the side may not be an option. You very well could end up just stuck there. In this case, I would still hit the hazard lights and then you may want to call the police department to let them know where you are and what has happened.

They're going to want to keep the flow of traffic moving, and will send an officer out to help you move your car to where it can be taken care of further.

Turn the car off and put it in park. If your car is still technically running, but it is spitting out massive amounts of smoke, or something like that, make sure your car is turned off so that you don't make the problem worse, and make sure that you put the car in park if you can so that the car doesn't decide to roll somewhere you don't want it too.

Do you have any friends or family members close by? – You're going to want to call around to check. They will be able to potentially come and get you or fix your car. Maybe both.

Does your car insurance offer some sort of assistance for situations like this, or are you a member of AAA? – AAA is an organization that you pay via a yearly membership fee. But if you are a member, and something bad happens to your car while you're out driving and you have nobody else around, you can give them a call and they will send one of their employees out to come and get you. Your car insurance may offer a similar type of service that you're unaware of. It's worth checking out anyway. AAA is pretty cheap annually, and it does serve as a tremendous peace of mind, particularly if you're a lone young girl traveling the country by yourself.

Don't just accept a ride from anybody though. Have I before? Yes. I've hitchhiked a number of times. But is it something that I recommend? No way, Jose. You never know who that person is that you're riding with in the car, and I have seen a number of rape and murders in my town as a result of people riding with hitchhikers. Just the other week a girl from my college was raped when hitchhiking "across campus". My town was rocked 2 years ago when another girl disappeared potentially with a hitchhiker. The unofficial rumor was that she was raped, cut into pieces, and then fed to the murderer's dogs.

So, don't hitchhike.

If none of the above options work out for you, you may just need to call a tow truck. – Tow trucks are absolutely no fun to call because they're expensive, but sometimes that's just life. You can't just leave your car there by the side of the road for the next week. You'll get a ticket otherwise. You need to get it taken care of. You need a car, and that car is your responsibility. In this case, being responsible may necessitate paying a tow truck.

The tow truck guy will not only take your car to the mechanic, but he will give you a lift there as well. You can probably expect a bill of about $100 depending upon where you are at.

If a stranger stops to ask if you need help...- I'm always incredibly leery of strangers pulling over to ask if I need help with car trouble. My wife broke down in West Virginia, called me, and then hung up when a stranger came to help her. She refused to answer her phone for the next several minutes. The rest of my coworkers at work were freaking out. "*Don't you watch movies?! That guy could be taking her off into the woods right now!*"

Yeah, it wasn't fun. I understood they were 100% right. Here she was stuck who knows where and the only bit of information I had was that a man had stopped to help her. Well, that's useful information. "*Yes, officer. We're looking for a man.*" That narrows it down to 50% of the population for us.

If somebody pulls over to help you at least send off a quick text to a trusted friend with the license plate number, make and model of vehicle, and what the helper looks like. You may think I'm being a bit paranoid here, but nobody expects to get kidnapped, raped, or murdered. Nobody wakes up in the morning thinking, 'Welp, I better get the most out of my last day on earth.'

But those things do happen. The least you can do is make it a little easier for authorities to find and rescue you should the worst happen.

How to Jump Start a Car

Batteries die.

Especially when it gets cold or you forget to turn your headlights off for the night. If either of these tends to happen around your car, then sooner or later you're going to be presented with the pleasant surprise of a dead battery. Even if it's not your own car, it's pretty cool to be able to help somebody else out of a sticky situation caused by a dead battery.

What you'll need are a set of jumper cables and a car that works.

Before going any further though I'll offer this disclaimer. A lot of newer cars have an electronic ignition system or are alternatively fueled (other than gasoline). Using jumper cables can damage these types of cars, so that's something that you're going to want to avoid. If that's the case with your car, you're screwed. You're just gonna have to get a ride somehow to get a new battery most likely.

If however the above doesn't apply to you then you're in luck.

1. Place both cars in PARK and ensure they're both turned off
2. Attach a red clip from the jumper cables on YOUR

batteries' positive terminal – This will be most likely marked by a '+' or the letters 'pos'.
3. Attach the other red clip to the positive terminal of the other car's battery
4. Attach one of the black clips to the negative battery terminal on the OTHER car's battery
5. Now connect the last black clip to a clean, unpainted metal surface under the car's hood.
6. Turn on the good car and run it for 2-3 minutes. The bad car should now be able to turn on as well.
7. Remove the cables in the reverse order of the way that you attached them.

Once you get your car started, don't turn it off. You're going to want to leave it on and potentially even drive it around for 15 minutes or so to build back your car battery's charge so that it doesn't die on you again. If despite doing this the car refuses to start again in the future then your battery is dead (it happens) and you're going to need to go out and buy a new one.

Pay very good attention to the order in which the cable clamps are attached. Going out of sequence could cause electric shock, damage to your car, or other bad things to happen.

Basic Car Maintenance

Unless you live in a very big city where everything you need is within walking/metro distance, you are going to need a car. However, cars break down and do require regular maintenance to keep them from breaking down in more expensive ways.

One of the most important things that you can do to keep your car up and running is to regularly change the oil. Just pay somebody to do this. It's not worth the time and energy to do this one yourself. You'll save maybe $5 by doing so, if even that. I swing into a Merchant's or Jiffy Lube real quick, and 20 minutes later I'm outta there.

I try to change my oil every 3000 miles or so. If you don't, gunk can build up in your engine, and then you end up ruining your engine which is a much more expensive repair (several thousand dollars) compared to just putting $90 in it every year.

When you go to one of these engine oil stores be prepared for them to tell you that your car is just about to fall apart and that you need to spend several thousand dollars in fluids for them to fix it for you. It's a crock. Don't fall for it. They know that you're young and inexperienced with cars, especially if you're a college-aged woman, and they'll attempt to nail you with unnecessary purchases.

All I ever do is get the oil changed. Occasionally I'll get

the air filter replaced as well, but only when they bring it out to me and I can visibly see that it's disintegrating. Car aficionados may hate me for this, but that's all I ever do and my cars have run great. I don't see the point in changing all of my engine fluids, brake fluids, transmission fluids, and everything else every other month. To me, it's just a waste of money. Sure, eventually you may want to do this, but I don't want to every 3 months.

Tires

You're going to want to make sure that your tires are in good shape as well. As time wears on your tires will wear down. When the tread all but disappears, your tires are considered 'bald'. Bald tires are dangerous. You no longer have much traction, and should the road be wet you stand a good chance of hydroplaning and flying off the road into another car, a guard rail, off a cliff, or into a tree.

Ending up paralyzed for the rest of your life because you refused to regularly check your tires is foolish. Imagine that being the cause of your wife being in a terrible accident. How'd you like to be responsible for that? Check the tires regularly.

The way to do this is the penny test. Take a penny and insert it into the tread with Abraham Lincoln's head upside down. If Abe's head disappears and is covered by the tread then your tires are still good. If the tread doesn't even begin to cover any of Abe's head then your tires are considered bald and you need to make it a top priority to get your tires replaced as soon as possible.

Every so often I'll make sure that I get my tires balanced as well. I do this maybe once a year. What this means is that the mechanic will make sure that the tires are properly balanced so that they do not cause uneven wear on the tires. Uneven wear means that the tire will vibrate, make noise, and not last near as long as it would otherwise.

It always cracks me up when I go to buy new tires and the mechanic asks if I would like them balanced. Uh, yes. I would like you to put the tires on correctly, please. Make sure that you do the same.

Regularly rotating your tires is another way that you can help to avoid uneven wear on them. No, this doesn't mean that you put your hand on the tire and spin it. You're going to have to go into the shop for this one. The mechanic will take the front tires and put them on the rear axle, and vice versa for the back tires. Once or twice a year is all I do for this.

Wiper blades

If you notice when you're driving in the rain that your wipers squeak, stutter, smear water, or fail to clear off your windshield then it is high time to get a new pair of wipers. Advance Auto Parts is my go-to for wiper blades, though any car store will sell them. If you go to Advance Auto Parts though they will not only tell you exactly what type of wipers you need, the different prices they have for your car's wiper blades, and they'll even install them for you.

I like Rain-X wiper blades the best. I feel they do a good job, and they seem to last for a good length of time. I'll often get the Rain-X wipes as well and use those to smear a protective hydrophobic chemical all over my windshield as well that makes it so the water just beads up and flows right off instead of smearing all over the glass too. These wipes aren't very expensive and they work absolutely fantastic.

Check your fluids

There are some fluids that you're going to want to regularly check to make sure that they are ok. Wiper fluid, antifreeze, and transmission fluid are all very easy to check and to fix as well should they start running low. A quick YouTube search will help you know where to check for these different fluids on your particular car.

What to Do if You Run Out of Gas

If you run out of gas while driving, your responses are going to be pretty similar to what would happen if you broke down on the side of the road. The only exception is that you may be able to actually do something about it here.

You always want to get your car out of the middle of the road should it stop working, and so your first order of business is going to be to do that.

If you're not out in the middle of nowhere and you actually remember seeing a gas station not too far back, then walking there to buy a canister filled with gas may be a good bet. Don't do this if you're stranded on a road where walking is illegal/could get you killed (such as an interstate), but if you're not that far it could be worth it.

Let's say that you are broken down in the middle of nowhere though. In that case, I would first start by calling nearby friends and family that may be able to give you a lift. If you don't have any options there, then calling AAA or even the police station would be your next best bet.

If a police officer ends up seeing you stuck on the side of the road as it is, they typically stop to make sure that everything is all right. Just be forewarned that running out of gas could potentially end up getting you a ticket.

It depends on the police officer, of course, but it's just something to be aware of.

How to Shop for a Car

I've shopped around for new cars a couple of times, and it's never something that I look forward to. In fact, I avoid it whenever possible, typically letting my wife handle finding vehicles for us. She actually does a much better job finding quality deals than I do anyway with that kind of stuff, so it works out.

The first couple of times that I went out to look for a car, all I really knew was that I wanted something with 25+mpg. You need to know a little bit more than that to find a proper car without getting price gouged.

What purpose will the vehicle serve you? If you need to haul kids, you probably want a minivan. If you do a lot of long drives or trips around town, a smaller car will probably serve you well. Live out in the country and mess with construction or livestock? A pickup is probably the right choice.

Figure out which type of vehicle will best suit the purposes that you need it for, and then go from there.

What are you willing to spend on gas? The higher the miles per gallon (mpg), the better. Higher mpg means less money you have to spend at Exxon. 30+mpg is good for a car, while you'll be lucky to find a truck that gets 18mpg.

Take a good hard look at your budget to figure out what you can afford here as well. Go back for the past 3-6 months or so and take a look at what you spent for gas on average. If you know what your current mpg is in your car then you can estimate how many miles you've driven in the past 3-6 months. Knowing this, you can now estimate how much you'll approximately pay for a vehicle with different gas mileage.

How old is the vehicle? If it's really old and the owner hasn't taken care of it like it was one of his own, then there's a possibility that the car could clunk out soon. I only look at vehicles for sale that are less than 10 years old. I don't have any science behind that one, but it's a number that makes me feel good about what I'm looking at. I feel comfortable shopping for a car that young.

How many owners has the vehicle had? The fewer owners the better. Multiple owners may mean that all of the preceding suckers bought a piece of crap that they quickly pawned off onto the next sucker. If people are getting rid of a car they just bought a year ago, something's up. Stay away from cars with these types of history.

Has the vehicle been in an accident? If so, there may be some hidden residual damage that the owner isn't even aware of. They may tell you that the only thing damaged was the rear fender, but you don't know for sure what the state of the frame and guts are until you've started driving the car for a while.

I only shop for vehicles that haven't been involved in an

accident. Now if you're handy with automotive repair, you can get some incredible deals on vehicles that have been in accidents and then fix them up yourself, but you better know what you're doing or you're just going to end up digging a money pit.

Did the previous owner smoke? If so, good luck ever getting the smell to come out. There's nothing like showing up to your job interview smelling like old cigarettes.

Even if you do manage to get the smoke smell out of the car, there's also something called third-hand smoke to be aware of. When the smoke from cigarettes and cigars settles, it leaves microscopic toxic particles deep within the fabric. Every time you then sit on where those particles have settled you poof them up into the air. Then you breathe them. Some research has shown that third-hand smoke may be just as dangerous as secondhand smoke.

Being hooked up to oxygen's no fun. Stay away from cigarette-y cars. And just because you can't smell the smoke doesn't mean that the danger is gone.

Is the car from the beach or where there's a lot of snow? In either of these cases, there can be a lot of corrosion that occurs on the underbody of the car. Both sand (from the beach) and ice melt that gets thrown on the road (from where it snows) will end up sticking to the bottom of the car.

If it's not washed off soon enough, over time this can lead to the entire bottom of your car becoming rusted out.

That's something you don't want. Avoid cars from these areas if you can.

Is the price comparable to what Kelley Blue Book says it should be? In my opinion, Kelley Blue Book is the gold standard for determining how much a car *should* cost. The website will give you a couple of questions about the car which you'll be able to enter, and then it will tell you if the person is charging you way too much or actually giving you a deal. I would not buy a car before checking out its average price from this source.

Are you buying from a dealer or from a private individual? – A dealer will typically have a higher sticker price for a car than an individual will. They have to pay rent on a big building. The private party doesn't. There's nothing wrong with either option (I've bought from both), but you do need to be aware of the potential pros and cons of both.

A dealership will typically offer you some sort of warranty on a car that you buy from them, oftentimes for 3 months. You can sometimes buy a larger warranty, but that is going to cost you a little bit more. This means that should you end up buying a lemon, you can get what you need to get fixed for free. However, with a dealership, you can often get a detailed history of what has happened with that car, including dates of service, car wrecks, and any other mechanical work that was done.

The best one of these that you can get is a CarFax. It'll tell you everything you could ever possibly want to know about the care that you are looking at buying, and it is a huge relief knowing what you've got there in front of you. A CarFax is peace of mind.

You don't have that option with an individual. You'll most likely get a much lower asking price from them, but you'll also get what you get. There's no warranty being offered by the old man down the street. The car may work great for him and then clunk out when you get it the next day. In a similar vein, he may not tell you the whole truth about the problems that the car has.

The car may have really bad issues with the tires staying in alignment, but if the old man doesn't want to tell you that you won't know that this is the case until you've driven the car for a couple of weeks.

The best way to work around this issue that I know of is to first ask lots of questions to an individual about the car history. Don't let 'Well, you didn't ask,' be an available excuse. The second option would be to find a mechanic and offer to pay them if they will take a look at the car before you buy it.

If you have a friend that can do this for you, then great. If you don't then politely tell the dealer that you are interested in the car (and you must be truly interested. Like, on the verge of buying it interested.), but that you'd like to have a mechanic look it over with both of you present before you buy it. Hopefully, the seller will say yes, and you will soon have a much better idea about what it is that you are buying.

That's all good, but where do I even begin to look for a car?

You could spend all day for several weeks driving around to all of the car dealerships in a 50-mile radius, but in my experience, it will only make it difficult to stay sane and not become an alcoholic. Just look online instead. If a reputable dealer truly wants to sell their car and they're smart, they'll have posted it online anyway. The best sources that I've found are these:

- **Cargurus.com** – I've found some really good deals on here, and this is actually my favorite site to car shop on. There are plenty of filters to find just what you're looking for, and it tells you to the exact dollar amount how much higher or lower the seller is asking compared to the average price of that particular vehicle.
- **Kbb.com** – Kelley Blue Book also has a pretty decent 'for sale' section where you can find what you're looking for as well. I don't like the layout of it as much as CarGurus, but you still may be able to find deals here that you couldn't elsewhere.
- **Autotrader.com** – My least favorite "vehicles-for-sale website", but my parents have found some good deals on trucks and other vehicles here. Lots of filters that will help you to find what you're looking for.
- **Craigslist** – Craigslist I always venture onto with a suspicious eye. I'm not sure why that's the case, but I suspect it has to do with the number of people out of town on there who have wanted to send their

friend to pay with a check for whatever I've posted on there for sale. You're predominantly dealing with private sellers here, and there's going to most likely be limited information on the cars that you may be interested in which will result in you actually having to drive out to find that car if you want it.

Every once in a while you'll hear about some lucky guy who goes on a treasure hunt on Craigslist and ends up with a brand new pickup for $3000 because somebody died or something, but these stories are incredibly rare.

Don't Buy a New Car!

Yeah, I know a lot of people are going to disagree with me on this. Hey, I even have family that disagrees with me on this, and strongly. Regardless though, I do not think that at this stage of the game it is in your best interest to buy a new car.

If you're 65, have saved adequately for retirement, have paid off your mortgage, and have some extra cash to buy the Thunderbird you've always wanted, then by all means have at it.

If you're 20-something, just starting out, wondering how you're going to pay rent each month, and have student loans, I think buying a new car is downright stupid.

The second you drive a new car off the lot it depreciates in value. You could drive the car off the lot, circle around town, swing back to sell it to the dealer and the amount you'll get will be a much smaller percentage of what you paid for it 20 minutes ago.

Do not buy a new car.

If you need a car buy a quality used one. Do a little bit of research. Find out what's good and what's not. Look at what you should expect price-wise. Search what's for sale in your community. After you've done all that, buy used.

You'll get much lower prices, the car can still be quality, and if you pay in cash (as you should) you won't have a monthly car payment with interest hanging over your head.

MONEY

There's no way around it. Money is a necessity of life. Perhaps no other material possession will impact your day-to-day life as will the presence (or lack) of money. Money is what allows one to pay the bills, purchase groceries, go on vacations, and pay for health insurance.

In short, you have to use it on a daily basis, and seeing that it will impact your life whether you want it to or not, you have to have some basic understanding of how it works and how to use it.

Here, we'll cover some of the basics of what school should have taught you about money.

How to Set Up a Bank Account (and why you should)

When I was in college I roomed with a guy (he's actually one of my best friends) who kept somewhere close to $40,000 in the tile ceiling of our dorm. He had recently won a court case and thought that would be a safe place to hide his cash.

Though nothing happened to it, that is by no means the ideal way to store your hard-won earnings. While I do believe that it is very important to keep some cash in your home and on your person at all times, I think that putting money in a bank account is a much wiser idea. Yes, savings and investments are very important too, and will actually earn you money via interest, but there needs to be a place where your funds can be easily accessed and stored.

A bank account is that place.

Not only are banks insured, meaning that if anything ever happens to that bank you are guaranteed to get your money back, but they serve as a convenient place to store very large amounts of cash that you need ready access to. Banks will earn you some interest as well, but the amount is so small that this point is basically moot.

If you want to make money off of your money, you don't place it in a bank. In that case, you'll place it in mutual funds, real estate, or businesses. However, you do need to have a savings account, you do need to have a checking account, and it is good to have a brick-and-mortar establishment to turn to in case you need to get a loan for a car or house someday.

A savings account should not be your primary form of savings. If you ask me, I say make your savings account your emergency account. Dave Ramsey, an absolutely fantastic financial advisor who was written scores of books on the subject, recommends that you keep an emergency fund of 3-6 months of living expenses on hand.

Now for somebody just starting out, I get it. That's a lot. But buying a house is a lot too. Buying a car is a lot. Buying a fridge is a lot. Yet people do it every day. How? By saving a little bit here and there slowly. Little strokes fell great oaks.

An emergency fund is a necessity. Put away even just 10% of each paycheck into your emergency fund, and you'll be surprised at how quickly it builds.

If you're on your own, you are now an adult. Mommy and Daddy aren't going to be there to bail you out of every situation, nor should they. Adults have responsibilities, and one of those things is to take care of themselves. An emergency fund is one of the ways that adults do that.

If your car dies and you suddenly need a new one, if your refrigerator suddenly needs repairs, or if you get injured somehow and cannot work, you are going to need a way to buy groceries, pay rent, and keep the lights on.

An emergency fund is the adult, responsible way to do that.

Having 3-6 months stored up in your savings account will give you enough of a buffer to hit the majority of surprises that get thrown your way. Once you get that money stored in your savings account, do your very best not to touch it as well unless you absolutely need it.

The other primary reason that you are going to need a bank account is to open a checking account. A checking account is going to be your primary way to pay bills, and odds are the primary way that you are going to be paid. If you pay bills online or via snail mail, the funds are going to be withdrawn from your checking account. If your employer opts to pay you via automatic deposit (which most employers do nowadays), then you are going to need a checking account.

A checking account is going to be the heart of your financial health. The majority of the transactions that you make are going to take place through here. So, make sure that you set up both when you go to set up a bank account.

Speaking about setting up a bank account, you are definitely going to want to shop around at different banks and see which one suits you best. Convenience, interest rates, and other variable factors are all going to be at play here.

If the bank you choose only has one location and is a 30-minute drive away, it becomes a hassle to get there regularly and your budgeting and emergency fund will suffer as a result. Choose something with multiple branches in convenient locations.

As we've mentioned before, interest rates are pretty much nonexistent at banks anymore. Your account isn't going to make you a ton of money. However, the more money that it *can* make you, however small that may be, the better.

A bank that gives 3% interest on your money is a better deal than one that gives 1.5% interest. If you have $10,000 in your bank account, a bank that gives you 3% interest will give you $300/year. The bank that gives you 1.5% interest will only give you $150/year. In case you failed math class, $300 is better.

In my own research, I've found that credit unions tend to give better interest rates than banks as well. So if you have a few credit unions around where you live, I highly recommend checking some of their rates out online.

As far as other variables go when choosing a bank, I try to find banks that are locally owned. Local guys tend to work better with you when there is an issue compared to the big banks in my experience. The local guy doesn't have near as much bureaucracy, red tape, and annoying policies to go through when you make a mistake, need a loan, or anything else.

After you take all of these variables into account and

have finally found what you believe to be the perfect bank in your area, how do you set up an account? Just call them and tell them that you'd like to, and they'll tell you what documentation and cash you need to bring with you to do so.

For a savings account, most banks require that you have a minimum amount deposited at all times (around $10 at my banks). You're going to need to bring this cash with you and potentially some other documentation as well. Just give them a call and they'll tell you what you need to do. Choosing the right bank is actually much more work than opening the accounts.

How to Maintain a Budget

Of all the 'adult' things (I should specify: *clean* adult things) that somebody out on their own for the first time ever needs to know I would argue that the knowledge of how to maintain a healthy budget is the most important.

Without the self-discipline and the know-how here, you can quickly end up going broke or worse. I've seen it all here. One friend of mine would go out and buy a new car every two years despite being deep in debt. Add his gambling addiction to this, and declaring bankruptcy came pretty quickly.

You have to be able to budget.

"Eh, as long as I make more than I spend I'll be ok."

Wrong.

You need to know where your money is going or you are going to end up wasting so much more of it than you thought. I'm also yet to meet somebody who had the "make more than you spend" mentality that ended up turning out ok in the end either.

So how do we keep a budget? There are many different methods out there, but I'll tell you what I've found to work for me the best.

Keep your receipts.

All of 'em. Not only do these help you to keep track of how much you've spent over the course of the month, but if you need to return anything, you'll want to get the full amount back, and in cash too. Without the receipt, you'll most likely get 60-70% of what you paid for the item, and there's a good chance that amount will be in the form of store credit (boooo.)

Also, receipts let you know what exactly it was that you spent money on. If you're like me, you'll get your credit card statement at the end of the month and see a bunch of random charges at Walmart and Lowes. Without your receipts, you'll have a slim to none chance of remembering exactly what it was that you bought that day.

Lastly, receipts allow you to prove that you paid a particular amount. A friend of mine was telling me one day how his wife keeps all of their restaurant receipts 'just in case'. Roughly once every month or so she would find that restaurants had conveniently increased the size of the tip that she had given them. It's funny how generous people can be with other people's money.

The receipt allowed her to prove to the restaurant manager that they had overcharged her for her bill, and she got her money back as a result. After hearing this I began to keep all of *my* restaurant receipts. Surely I wouldn't find people to be doing the same thing to me. I mean, aren't people basically good?

Within 3 weeks I'd noticed that a waiter at a local Mexican restaurant had conveniently upped the size of his tip.

So, keep your receipts.

Get a piece of paper and categorize everything you *need* to spend money on.

For most people, rent, car payments, phone bills, electricity, water bill, groceries, gas for your car, car insurance, and student loans will be something that they have to pay on a monthly basis.

These are the bills that you *have* to pay every month or you'll be living on the street. Find out how much on average you pay for all of these things every month and make absolutely certain that you have those funds available in your bank when the time comes.

Now categorize all of the things that you don't necessarily need, but you would like to work towards or do enjoy having.

This may be a vacation to Palm Springs, a new car, music lessons, your dog Duke or whatever. Without budgeting for these things, you're going to be spending most of your evenings sitting at home staring at a wall.

Average a couple of your past paychecks to figure out approximately how much you're going to make per week.

For most people, their paycheck isn't going to vary very much week to week (waiters and salesmen may be the exception). Either way, you need to know approximately how much bacon you're going to bring home each week.

Knowing all this, now you need to know how much of your paycheck should go to each category.

So if I know I need $500/month for rent and I make $3000/month, then my rent costs around 17% of my monthly pay. So, 17% of each paycheck needs to be set aside for rent.

How do you set it aside?

One method I like is the envelope system.

In this method, you'll have a separate envelope filled with the allotted amount of cash for each category in your budget. Studies show that when we spend with cash instead of with a card we spend less money overall. We develop an emotional attachment to cash that we don't to a credit card. When we can visually see our money disappearing it makes us think twice before spending it.

If keeping stacks of cash-filled envelopes around your house sounds like too much work though, I'd recommend checking on how much you've spent on various categories at least once a week. This will help to give you a guideline as to how much you've spent on each category, and how much you have left.

That's the gist of budgeting, and there are many different ways to keep an accurate account of where you are currently at financially.

Sure there are apps out there that will do all of the budgeting grunt work for you, but I'm still a little timid about trusting these things. Often, they want to be hooked up with your bank account info and credit card information. That alone spooks me out. As history has proven, hackers can access pretty much whatever they want that's stored on software, and I don't like the idea of my information being that much easier for somebody else to get a hold of.

Secondly, I like being a little more present with the current state of my finances. I want to see each individual charge and write it down in my ledger that I have to help to ensure that I better remember just how much money is going where.

I have buddies that use those budgeting apps and absolutely love them, claiming that they save them a ton of time and money, but the choice is ultimately up to you. Weigh the pros and cons and decide what you would be most comfortable with.

You're going to want to do a little more in-depth reading on this one than space allows here, so I highly recommend Dave Ramsey's *Total Money Makeover.* He's the best financial advisor out there that I've found and he has a score of great books out there that do an incredible job of explaining what most makes a very confusing subject.

What to Do With Debt

Debt sucks. I'm working through it right now. My wife and I are still paying off our student loans. Whether you are working off credit card bills, car payments, college loans, or whatever, debt leaves you a slave to the lender.

Combine the melancholy that comes with writing yet another check for that debt yet another month with the fact that interest seems at times to be an ever-growing snake and you'll further understand why debt sucks.

You need to do what you can to get out of it as quickly as you can.

Compounding interest can result in your literally paying thousands of dollars more for an item than you would have in the first place. When we bought our first house I can remember looking at the interest payment predictions. When all was said and done, we were going to end up paying roughly double what our house was worth over the course of 30 years thanks to the interest payments.

The key to wriggling out from underneath this rock is to chip away at the principal of the loan as much as you can and as often as you can.

Financial planner and author Dave Ramsey has an

approach to this that I really like. He calls it the Snowball Method.

Let's say you are in debt for three different objects: your student loans, your car payment, and your credit card bill.

- Student Loans – $37,000
- Car Payment – $6578
- Credit Card – $600

Each of these objects is going to have a minimum payment required per month. That means you have to pay at least X dollars each month for that particular loan. Using the snowball method you pay the minimum payment each month for everything but the *smallest* loan. The smallest loan you attack like a cheese pizza after a backpacking trip. You do everything you can to absolutely devour it. You scrimp and save and put as much towards it as you can until you have annihilated it.

Now that the credit card bill is gone, you take the amount you were paying towards it each month and apply it to the next smallest loan, in this case, the car payment. So now student loans are still getting the minimal payment, but the car payment is getting its minimal payment and what you were paying per month for the credit card. On top of this, you now do all the scrimping and saving that you can to pay off the car as quickly as you can. This cycle repeats itself until you are debt-free.

The theory here is that by paying off the smallest loan first, you not only create some mental freedom by getting something off of your plate, but you get yourself excited in seeing that you have eliminated a source of your debt. This excitement then spills over into the next area that you are trying to conquer.

Some people would object and say that they want to pay the loan with the highest interest first, but according to Ramsey's experience, he says that people tend to burn out that route. Human psychology wins in the end, and the best way to beat human psychology in this instance is to use the snowball method.

For further reading here, I highly recommend Dave Ramsey's *Total Money Makeover*. His *Financial Peace University* is about a 2-month course that greatly helped my wife and me when we were first starting out and may help you as well. It cost about $70 but was worth every penny. Dave Ramsey has written several other books on the subject of money management as well and is widely viewed as one of the best, if not the best, financial advisor out there for the common man.

Understanding Compounding Interest

After talking with a number of my friends throughout college, and just from watching the lives unfold of those around me I've discovered that the majority of people have absolutely no idea what the ramifications of compounding interest are.

This is a big thing, and it can either be an incredible tool or an unforgiving curse. You need to know not only what compounding interest is, but how you can use it to your advantage as well. Any time that you take out a loan, you have what is called the principal of the loan. Let's say you just took out a $10,000 loan for college. The principal of the loan is that $10,000. That's the original amount of money that the loan was worth.

Compounding interest is what gives that loan the capacity to grow into an angry grizzly bear. It's how the person that gave you that loan makes money. Let's say that for that $10,000 college loan the interest rate was 5% and compounded annually.

By the end of 1 year, you would have accrued $500 in interest on that loan that you would have to pay back in addition to the original $10,000. By 5 years, $2762 worth of interest would have accumulated. By 10 years, $6288 worth of interest would have accumulated. By 20 years

$16,532 worth of interest would have accumulated. And just to further make my point, by 50 years the interest alone on that original $10,000 would have been $104,673.

That's a lot of money.

Now of course that example isn't factoring in your making regular payments on that loan or anything else, but the point remains: compounding interest doesn't stop. It will keep growing whether you like it or not, so you must do what you can to attack it as quickly as possible. By not only making regular payments but by paying extra on top of the minimum monthly payment you help to ensure that you not only stay on top of the ever-growing interest but that you whittle away at the principal of the loan too.

The smaller the principal of the loan, the slower the compounding interest will expand. That is why you want to do everything that you can to pay off any loans that you may have as quickly as possible. If you don't, you quite literally become a slave to your loans and you will end up paying thousands of dollars more than you would have had to if you had paid them off quickly.

Sure, it may require some sacrifices to defeat compounding interest, but guess what? That's part of being out on your own now. That responsibility is part of being an adult. And if you don't like the idea of becoming a captive of your creditors then better yet, don't pay for things with loans! Just make do without and save up the cash in the meantime to pay for that thing in one lump sum.

Sure, this may not work for a house at this point in the game for you, but it will definitely work for that phone, car, TV, or whatever else out there that you need to have. Delayed gratification can save you a lot of headaches and heartaches in the long run.

Just in case you ever want to calculate the compound interest of a loan for yourself, here's the formula:

Compounding interest = $[P(1+i)n] - P$

P = principal, I = nominal annual interest rate in percentage terms, and n = number of compounding periods

You don't really need to know how to do this by hand, as there are plenty of interest calculators online that will probably give you an even better picture of what you're in for, but it is kind of fun to know how to do it

So, now that we've talked about how compounding interest can be absolutely terrifying, how can we use it as a tool to benefit us?

The answer?

By using it to save money.

The sooner that you start saving money, the longer it has to grow. And as we saw from the $10,000 loan example above, given enough time with compounding interest your savings can grow exponentially.

That's pretty cool, huh? Waking up one day to get some money out of your retirement account, and there's a ton there that wasn't there initially.

Why You Should Shop Around Before Making Big Purchases

You want to know what's a bad feeling?

I'll tell you what's a bad feeling.

Going to the store and dropping 3 grand on a washer/dryer combo at Sears and then finding out that the same washer/dryer combo was $700 cheaper at Lowe's 8 days later is a bad feeling.

When it comes to making *big* purchases, you know the ones that kind of make you stress out a little, you need to make sure that you do your research. By not doing so you can literally waste thousands of dollars a year that would be much more useful being applied to student loans, rent, savings, or an awesome vacation.

As a general rule of thumb, I've found that I tend to get a better picture of how the marketplace is when I shop around *at least* 3 separate locations. If you take the first bid you get, you're gonna get screwed. You don't want that. So shop around.

It gives you a better idea of what the marketplace is like for the particular item/service is that you need, as well as gives you an idea as to who is high-priced in your area.

For example, a few years ago my check engine light

came on in my car. I took it to AutoZone to get the free readout and discovered that I needed work done on my transmission. The first two mechanics that I called told me that I was going to need my transmission completely rebuilt which was going to cost several thousand dollars.

The car wasn't even worth several thousand dollars, so as I began to stress out I decided to call another mechanic to see what he would say. Turns out I needed my shift solenoid replaced. He fixed my car for around $100.

Had I not called around I would have ended up wasting thousands of dollars on an issue that was relatively easy to fix. Make sure that you shop around.

My other piece of advice with big decisions would be to not rush into anything. Don't just walk into a furniture store and buy a several-thousand-dollar couch on a whim. Sleep on it first. It's amazing how just over the course of one night the initial adrenalin rush can wear off and you'll be able to think logically again. You'll be able to make a much better decision in the morning after you've had some time to ponder over whether that purchase is the best for your current situation or not.

How to Negotiate

Some people love to negotiate, and others do not. Entire books have been written on the subject, and I don't have the space to give a comprehensive guide to what truly is an art form. But if you stick to these main pointers you will improve your odds of landing a solid deal immensely.

1) **Don't enter the negotiation with your absolute best deal**. – It's a negotiation, and the other party is going to attempt to negotiate you for something less. If you come in at your rock bottom you're only going to either end up losing the deal or accepting a crappy deal. Give yourself some wiggle room.

2) **Don't lie or play games** – Be 100% honest with whoever you're dealing with. You would want somebody to do the same with you and you don't want to earn the reputation of being a crook.

3) **Look for a win–win outcome** – Believe it or not, the person on the other side of the deal wants to end up walking away from this deal feeling like they weren't just screwed over. By putting an offer on the table where both parties win, you'll help the deal to run much more smoothly and quickly.

4) **Create a relationship with the other party** – Look for what you have in common with the other party and create a quick bond over that commonality. People have a

hard time confronting somebody who they don't deem to be a complete stranger. Go into the negotiation at ease and you will help to ensure that the opposing party does not enter with their guard up.

5) **Think outside the box** – There may be alternative ways to ensure that both parties end up getting what they want. You just have to be creative. Don't assume that there is only one way to seal a deal.

6) **Ask for what you want** – Being timid has no place in a negotiation. The other party cannot read your mind, and is not going to want to be overly generous. Ask for what you want from the get-go and move on from there.

7) **Do your homework on the situation** – If you are attempting to buy a used truck, it helps to know how much those particular trucks typically run for, if they tend to have issues, and if there is a similar offer in the next city over. By knowing the facts surrounding a situation you not only help to prevent yourself from being screwed over, but you help to ensure that you get as good a deal as possible.

8) **Don't take it personally** – When the other person says something negative about what you're offering, don't take it personally. Doing so just runs up your emotions, and your emotions are not your friend when you are trying to negotiate. This is a time that you need to think logically and with your brain rather than your heart.

9) **Don't give without getting something in return** – You know what happens when you give a mouse a cookie?

Carry Cash

In a world filled with credit cards, why would you ever need to carry cash again? Doesn't it just make your wallet uncomfortable? Doesn't it put you at risk of being mugged? Doesn't it increase your chance of losing your money?

The answer?

Nope. Not really.

Carrying cash is the smart thing to do. Let me start off with this story. Back in my life BC (before cash) my wife and I went to a farmer's market. My wife loves kettle corn, and we waited in line to get her some while. After getting to the front we discovered that they didn't take credit cards. My wife was pretty sad about it. I didn't like seeing her that way, and so since then, I've always carried some cash with me.

Yeah, yeah, I know that's a super silly story. But it illustrates a point that you may have missed. You may not always be able to rely upon your credit card to buy yourself something. If a store's credit card software malfunctions, power goes out, or a whole host of other what-ifs happen, then you could be left standing there absolutely screwed if you don't carry at least some cash.

What do you do if you're just about out of gas (a foolish

position to put yourself in, by the way) and the only gas station for miles doesn't have a working card reader? You're screwed. What do you do if you take a girl out on a date, and the card reader at the restaurant is broken? You're out of luck.

I'm not saying that you need to walk around carrying $800 in your wallet, I think that's foolish too, but carrying $100 in various denomination bills is a fairly secure amount to ensure that you will be able to tackle whatever financial curveballs get thrown your way while you are out and about.

I also think that it is wise to keep a larger amount of cash hidden and locked tight within your house. First, you never know when some type of random financial issue is going to get thrown your way that can only be solved by cash. If that something happens near the weekend (which they tend to do in my experience) then the banks are most likely not going to be open, and you're screwed again.

Secondly, keeping some cash at hand at home helps to ensure that perchance there is a major power outage in your region you will still be able to buy gas, groceries, water, and whatever else you may need. Longer-term power outages are fairly common. Ask anybody you know. I can just about guarantee you that they can remember at least two times when the power went out for a couple of days. If this happens and you don't have the resources at hand that you need, cash is going to be what you need to get them.

All About Credit Cards

A credit card can be a great tool, but it can also be a powerful temptation. According to Dave Ramsey, the best financial planner I know of, you not only don't need one but shouldn't have one if you want to have a healthy budget.

In my experience, you do have to have one.

When my wife and I first got married neither of us had ever had a credit card. As a result, we had no credit built up. This made it pretty much impossible for us to work with certain companies. We also barely managed to rent a vehicle on our honeymoon. The company didn't accept debit or cash. It was only after I told our situation to a manager 30 minutes later that he was willing to work with me.

Don't do that to yourself.

If you feel that you possess enough self-control, I think that a credit card can be an excellent way to not only build credit but get you some pretty sweet perks as well.

Most credit cards out there have some sort of reward system. Some cards will give you cash back for every dollar you spend, some will give you airline miles, some will give you hotel nights, and some will give you reward points.

If you really do your research, you can end up with a free round-trip flight somewhere within the course of a year just by buying the things that you're already going to buy anyway.

I've had four different credit cards in my life. All but one had a reward system. Out of the other three, one gave me a discount at one of my wife's favorite retailers, one gave me cash back, and the other collected airline miles for me which I could then redeem for plane tickets.

Find out what works best for you, and then apply for just ONE if you think that it's a good idea.

I don't think that you need more than one, and if you do get more than one it's going to take that much longer for your rewards to actually accumulate.

The main thing about credit cards is this though: do NOT get a credit card if you are not going to pay it off in full at the end of every month. If you only pay a portion of your credit card statement even once in my opinion, you are not ready for a credit card and you need to cancel it now.

If you don't you are going to get slammed by sky-high interest rates which will cause you to pay even more for those items you purchased in the long run.

Studies do show that people spend more money when they buy everything with a credit card when compared to cash. Cold hard cash is something that you have an emotional connection to. When you have a wallet full of cash it makes you think twice about buying something. You'll be more likely to ask yourself if you really need it.

Why?

Because it's sad to terminate your relationship with all those Founding Fathers. When you visually see your money leaving, you become more hesitant to want to spend it.

A credit card doesn't do this for you. There is no emotional value here. You think, 'Hey, I can just pay for this later!', and then you do. In some cases you pay in more ways than one for that item later.

So then where do I stand? I just told you I think a credit card is a necessary evil many times but then told you how horrible it is on your budget.

The choice is really up to you. If you have the discipline to pay the bill off every month then I think a credit card is a good way to build up your credit, give you a bit of an emergency hedge, and get some cool rewards.

If you don't have the discipline, then I think using a credit card is just a way to get yourself in trouble.

You know yourself. Do what seems wise.

How to Write a Check

Until my very first bill showed up in my mailbox, I had never actually written a check before in my life. Sure, I'd had a checkbook for years, but why would I use that when I could always just swipe a card? No one had ever taught me what to do with it before.

But now things were different. I was an official adult. And as a result, I needed to learn how to write a check. After staring at a blank rectangular piece of paper and doing a few Google searches, I finally figured out that it actually wasn't as daunting of a task as I had originally thought.

Checks rely on carbon paper. – That's paper that writes on the paper underneath of it to record an exact copy for somebody else. In this case, that person is you. Before you write a check, place something hard underneath the check *and* carbon copy, such as a magazine, folded piece of paper, or whatever.

Otherwise, that one check that you write will copy over to the next 5-6 checks underneath it which can be incredibly frustrating when you need to look back through your old records later on.

On the line immediately adjacent to the words "Pay to the Order Of", you're going to write who you are actually paying the check to. – So, if this is a check for Verizon, write "Verizon" here. If this is a check to your brother, write your brother's name there. Whoever is actually getting the money is who you're going to write the check out to.

Write the current date on the line immediately above the word "Date" which appears in the upper right-hand corner. – Easy 'nuff.

There's a box on the right side of the check with a dollar sign to the left of it. Write the amount that the check is for here. – Use numbers. So if you owe $237.75, fill it out to look exactly like that.

There's a line on the check immediately *under* the words "Pay to the Order Of". Here you are going to spell out the amount the check is for. – So for the above case of a bill for $237.75, you would write "two hundred thirty-seven and 75/100."

You don't have to write the word "dollars" as it will appear already at the end of this line. The fraction that you are going to write designates the cents. 100 cents = 1 dollar, so if you're paying 75 cents then you would write 75/100. If you have 33 cents to pay then you would have 33/100 at the end of this line. Or 00/100 if the amount due is right on the dollar.

In the bottom left corner of the check is going to be a line that says "For" beside it. This line is really for yourself more than anything. – Just write what you are paying the check for here to remind yourself later on what that check went out for.

In the case of some bills, you'll want to write your specific account number with that company here to speed up the payment process. It's not absolutely necessary, but companies say it helps them out a lot, so I do it. Your specific account number, receipt number, or whatever other name they have for your specific purchase/account will be somewhere on the paper bill you received in the mail.

Lastly, in the far right corner of the check, there is a line. Here is where you will sign your name to the check to verify that you indeed wrote it.

And that's it! That is how you write a check! If you ever run out of these just give your bank a call and let them know. They'll get you some more, and will probably have you pick them up at the actual bank. However, I would make it a point to order more checks well before you get down to the last one. You don't want to get to the point where you have to write a check to pay the garbage man, but you're out, and it'll be a week before the new ones come in.

What if I mess up?

If you mess up on a check (for example, by writing the wrong recipient in the line) then you're going to have to start over. I write the word 'void' in big capital letters across the length of the check and then rip out the check and shred it. That way nobody is able to get access to my routing number and account number from the check, and the word 'void' is on one of the ledgers within my checkbook, letting me know that that particular number check was never used.

Checks have numbers.

If you look in the top right-hand corner you'll see it listed. This makes it so that it is easy to identify which check paid what. That way if you go to check your online banking account and see a $45 check withdrawal without a recipient name online, but know that it was check #2589 that paid it then you can easily look back through your old records to see who that $45 went to.

How and When to Tip

This is often a source of frustration for me. What used to be a simple 10% for good service has now grown exponentially. Not only are people expecting a much larger tip now, but more people are expecting tips now than ever before. Look closely enough and you'll find tip jars everywhere, even for jobs that have no business asking for one (in my opinion).

So to start with, who is it customary to tip?

Waiters, bartenders, barbers/hairdressers, and pizza delivery guys are the only people who I give tips too. Some people will say that I'm stiffing a whole host of workers, but if they're getting paid a decent wage per hour, I don't feel that I *have* to tip. Congratulations. You did your job.

For all jobs that seem to lie in the gray such as valet parking attendants and the like, I just do what I need to do myself, and save myself the cash. Sorry, I'm broke. I don't have the means to tip every other person that I come into contact with.

It's only for the jobs that rely on tips that I regularly give one too. I give one to my barber just as a way to say thanks and because I'm secretly terrified she'll give me a terrible haircut the next time I swing by because of a lousy tip.

How much to tip though? Anywhere between 15-20% of the bill is now considered a respectable tip, and you should use the degree of professionalism the staff exhibited and the amount of trouble you put them through to determine where in that range your tip should fall. That doesn't mean you have to tip within that amount.

If the service is absolutely terrible, and the waiter is a jerk, I may not tip at all. Typically I always leave something, but it may be incredibly low if you're lousy at your job. On the flip side, if the service and staff absolutely blow your expectations out of the water, tipping higher than 20% on occasion may be something that you want to do as well.

It's really up to you on this one, and based on the experience you had with that particular business.

Couponing

What I once viewed as a Sunday afternoon activity for soccer moms I have now learned to embrace. Couponing will save you hundreds if not thousands of dollars throughout the course of a year. My wife and I use coupons all the time, and we both think that you should too. It doesn't take that much effort to get them, and you'll appreciate the chunk of change that they allow you to keep in your pocket. Here is where we get them from:

Newspapers – We don't subscribe to a newspaper anymore, but often are able to pick up one here or there. Newspapers are often filled with glossy inserts that will save you money, particularly the Sunday newspaper. Newspapers often have an option where you can subscribe solely on Sundays just for this reason. Yeah, there's a bit of an upfront cost, and you have to weigh the cost versus the benefit here, but they can still be a great place to find savings.

Retailmenot.com – We do a fair amount of shopping online, as do most people. If you've signed up on an email list for any online retailer such as Old Navy, Shutterfly, Fandango, or whatever you've probably noticed that some of those emails contain coupon codes to enter on your next purchase. Coupons sent to your email box? That's good. The problem is that you will literally get thousands of these emails, filling your inbox to the brim and forcing you to sift through an immeasurable pile of garbage to find the gold.

So instead, I just use retailmenot.com. All I have to do is type in the site I'm shopping on, and RetailMeNot will let me know if they have any promotional codes for that site or not. Usually, they do, and usually, you actually have a list of different promotions that you can sift through to find out which one will save you the most money. You click on the promotion you want, and then the code will pop up. Enter the code into the shopping site, and you'll get a discount.

Groupon – Groupon is good for online shopping, restaurants, travel, and a lot of other things. We have the most luck using Groupon for restaurants. We like to take mini-vacations for 1-2 nights where we spend as little money as possible. We'll use Groupon beforehand to search for restaurants at our destination that have coupons posted on the site.

With Groupon, you have to actually pay for the coupon, but you still end up saving money. For example, I could buy a half-price pizza at Vinny's Italian Pizzeria Factory online at Groupon, but if I had bought that same pizza in the store I would have had to pay full price.

We've found some absolutely incredible deals on travel via Groupon as well. Anytime you can find a 1-week tour through Europe where airfare is included for a total of $800/person, you've found a deal.

This method takes a little more forethought, but it can literally save you thousands of dollars if you use it consistently.

How to Save for Retirement

I know that retirement is probably the last thing on your mind right now, but please please please please PLEASE start saving for retirement right now!

I know the excuses. I've been there. You don't have any money right now. You're barely making it by as it is. Yes, I get all that, life happens. And guess what? You'll *always* find an excuse to not start saving for retirement today. You just had a baby, you just moved, you just bought a car, your refrigerator just broke.

Life happens. But so does retirement.

My job puts me in contact with retired people all day long. I get to see both sides of the equation very visibly. I see the couples who get to take fun trips together, can give their grandkids cool gifts, can afford their medications, can go out to eat if they want to. I also see the couples who wear the same clothes they've had for 40 years, skip medications on certain days of the week to save pills, cut napkins in half to save money, haven't had a vacation since they quit working, and constantly stress about how they're going to make ends meet next month all because they didn't save enough money.

You have to save for retirement. Those that do not set themselves up for some very difficult living situations in the future.

Even if you're only saving 5% each paycheck to it, at least it's *something*. So, here are my recommendations for saving for retirement:

Find a good financial advisor in your area. Merrill Lynch, Wells Fargo, and a host of other financial advisor will litter your city, I guarantee it. Do a quick Google search, and find one you trust. From there you need to give them a call and set up an appointment.

The financial manager will talk you through the various ways that you can begin to save for retirement. I highly recommend opening a Roth IRA. With a Roth IRA, you are not taxed for the interest that you accumulate on your account until you retire. This can save you a lot of money in the long run.

Invest in mutual funds. There's a lot of debate on this, but I really think that mutual funds are the best bet for a young investor. Regular stocks and bonds are just too volatile in my opinion. They go up and down at the drop of a dime.

A mutual fund is a collection of stocks from various companies. With a normal stock, you may have $10,000 invested in just Apple. But if Apple has a crappy year, your stock could easily drop to well below $10,000. And what happens if Apple goes under? You lose all $10,000.

That's no fun.

A mutual fund gives you a hedge of protection. It's a collection of stocks. I may have $10,000 invested in one mutual fund but that mutual fund has stocks from

Apple, Coca-Cola, McDonald's, Johnson & Johnson, Merck, Walmart, Domino's, Verizon, and much more. If Apple tanks, there's a minuscule effect on my investment. I have $10,000 invested in that one mutual fund, but maybe only 2% of it is invested in Apple stock.

Mutual funds are a much safer bet in my opinion, and they still give great returns. Ask your financial advisor to give you some of the names of ones that he really likes.

If your employer has a retirement savings plan as part of your benefits package, take full advantage of it. Most employers will give their full-time employees a package where they will match what you save (normally up to 3%).

So if you agree to have 3% of your paycheck automatically deducted and invested in a mutual fund that the company furnishes, then the company will *give* you an additional 3%. It's free money, and you'd be stupid not to take it.

What is Your Credit Score?

Your credit score is a number that is ascribed to you between the numbers 300-850. Your credit score lets businesses and potential lenders know how trustworthy you are financially. In other words, if you take out that loan for a truck, car, TV, whatever are you likely to pay them back? The higher the credit score, the more trustworthy you are deemed to be.

You want a high credit score not only to get the loan in the first place but because higher credit scores often get you lower interest rates on loans as well compared to somebody who has a low credit score. This in turn means that you will spend less money to repay the loan compared to the person with the low credit score.

There are actually a number of different credit scoring systems, but the FICO scoring system is the one that is most common and is the only one that you need to worry about. As long as it is high, the rest will be high as well.

The algorithm for a FICO credit score relies upon 1) length of credit history; 2) current debt; 3) payment history; 4) new credit; and 5) types of credit used.

If you're just starting out and have never had a credit card before in your life, then there's a good chance that your credit score is going to be abysmally low even if you've made prompt payments on everything you've ever bought in your life.

To keep your credit score high all you have to do is pay your bills on time, not continually load yourself down with new debt, and do this consistently.

How to Pay Bills

When I first moved out on my own, I couldn't wait for my first bills to show up in the mail. Up until that point I had never had a car payment. My phone bill, I paid to my dad in cash. I didn't have a credit card. Everything that I had ever bought before up until that point had been in cash.

When that first electric bill came in the mail though, I had the opposite reaction that most do when they see bills. I had *arrived*. That little white envelope in my hand with a cellophane panel was my official diploma saying that I was now an adult. I had entered the "real" world.

It wasn't long afterward that I no longer gleefully looked forward to the beginning of every month when bills would pile up in my mailbox.

I would argue that most bills are still paid via snail mail. You write a check, you fill out the billing slip, and you put everything into your mailbox.

1. Analyze the bill to make sure that everything looks correct. You want to make sure that the bill is actually for you (sometimes they can get sent to the wrong address, and it's never fun to pay Mr. Brown's water bill)
2. Write the check for the amount required
3. Fill in any additional information that the billing slip may require (oftentimes, this is just the 'amount

paid'. However, some bills will want other information as well.)
4. Insert the check, billing slip, and any additional required materials into the envelope. Make sure that the address is visible.
5. Put a stamp on it, and send it out!

That's really as complicated as it gets when it comes to paying your bills. Now, some places are going to be different. Most large companies that I've dealt with (e.g. Verizon, gas companies, electric companies) do offer the option for an automatic withdrawal. This means that once a month when the bill is due there will be an automatic withdrawal from your bank account for the amount that you owe the company.

I don't like this option. It feels a bit invasive to me, and if the company makes a mistake and overcharges you, they already have your money and you're screwed. You can get it back, but it will most likely be in the form of credit with that company and require several long-winded phone calls.

Some companies also offer the ability to pay your bills online. This will save you a stamp, and the payment typically goes through instantaneously so you don't have to worry about the mailman delivering your bill in time. Just make sure that you print off the billing statement so that you have proof that you paid the bill for that month.

Just make absolutely sure that you have that money in your account on the day that they withdraw it! If you don't, that creates a whole host of issues that you don't want to deal with. If you don't have the necessary funds then your bank may payout the bill but hit you with an over-withdrawal fee (which can be pretty hefty and is often applied every day that you are overdrawn). OR the bank may refuse to give the funds over (rightfully so), and your payment to the company that you owe will not go through.

When this happens, interest may be applied to your account, you may get slammed with a late fee in addition to your bill, and the company may shut off your service (a pleasant surprise to find out you no longer have electricity, water, or TV after a long day of work), or there may be a combination of all of these. So make sure you have the necessary funds in your account on withdrawal day!

For the same reasons, you want to make sure that you are paying your bills on time as well. Get a cheap calendar somewhere (OfficeMax has them) and make yourself a reminder of what days different bills are due. And don't forget that if they're due on a certain day of the week it may take the mail a few days to get there in time. Think ahead!

How to do Taxes

I just finished doing this one the other night, so it seems like a good time to write about this. Every year, like it or not, you need to file your taxes. If you don't, the IRS will find out. And you don't want the IRS to find out if you don't like hefty fines and potential jail time. So, file your taxes.

Most of the people that I talk to file their taxes somewhere around the month of January. For the last 4 years (it's 2017 as I write this), the due date for taxes to be filed has fallen in the month of April. This in no way means that you want to wait until the very last minute to file your taxes though. Unforeseen things can happen to keep your taxes from being filed on time, so make sure that you get them done as soon as you possibly can.

There are really only two final destinations with filing your taxes. Either you get a refund, meaning the government will give you a check (which in some cases can be a few thousand dollars), or you'll have to pay the government more in taxes. Most people just starting out will get a refund.

You also need to know that you have to file your taxes at both the state and federal levels. That means that you have to file taxes with the U.S. government, as well as with the state that you live in.

In order to complete your taxes, you're going to need a heinie-load of paperwork. Just get mentally prepared for that. Typically, by the end of January, all of the documentation that you will need for that year will be mailed to your address. If you had a job somewhere (and you should), you'll receive something called a W-2.

A W-2 details how much money you made last year, as well as how much you contributed to social security, what part of your paycheck you were taxed, as well as other information. If you went to a college, university, or another form of higher education, you may have another form sent your way called a 1098-T. If you paid a mortgage, paid student loans, or made interest from a bank account, you will have the paperwork sent to you for those things as well.

Once you have all of the paperwork that you need, you have to decide how you want to complete your taxes. For years I had my dad complete my taxes for me. He successfully ran a local business, had completed his own taxes for years, and was pretty good at knowing what to do with them.

If you have a friend or family member that knows how to file taxes, great! If they are competent, they may save you a little bit of money by giving you the opportunity to complete your taxes for free. However, I would make sure that particular family member or friend knew what they were doing. Taxes are nothing to screw around with. They are incredibly complex, and incorrect information could cost you thousands of dollars, or worse.

If you don't have somebody who knows how to do taxes though, no worries. There are plenty of other companies out there that would be more than happy to help you file your taxes – for a nominal fee.

H&R Block, Jackson Hewitt, Liberty Tax Service, local accountants, and TurboTax are just a few of the tax services that you can purchase to help you navigate through the incredibly complicated world of filing your annual taxes.

H&R Block and Jackson Hewitt are the two most popular brick-and-mortar stores to get your taxes filed, in my experience. They'll typically charge you by the hour, with the price varying as well based on how complex your personal tax situation is (it's different for everybody). If you're just starting out on your own, your taxes probably aren't going to be too complicated though. It's when you're self-employed, own rental properties, or sold quite a bit on the stock market that things get (more) difficult.

The benefit of going to a brick-and-mortar store is that the person you are working with will potentially have years of experience behind their back. They'll have worked with hundreds of other clients just like you, and will know how to get you as many deductions as possible (read they get you more money back). They'll tell you exactly what you need to do, tell you exactly what paperwork to have handy, will file your taxes for you, and will be able to answer any questions that you have as well.

The only con here is the price. They really can't give you a quote because pricing varies so much, but for somebody just starting out it shouldn't be anything more than $250, and hopefully, it will be much less.

If you'd rather fill your taxes out yourself, you are going to need some form of tax software to walk you through what you need to do. TurboTax and H&R Block are the most well-known. You can pick the software package up at Walmart, or you can just go to their respective websites (which I've been told is cheaper) and purchase the software online.

I've used both TurboTax and H&R Block's tax software. My opinion? Choose TurboTax, and avoid H&R Block's software like the plague. TurboTax has the decency to actually dumb everything down for you as much as possible (that sounds condescending, but trust me, you'll appreciate the condescension later). H&R Block doesn't. It's as if they assume that you already have a clue what you're doing, and unless you have a good bit of experience filing taxes, you don't.

The software will walk you through your taxes, asking questions that are relatively straightforward (e.g., "Did you buy a house? Did you pay medical expenses? Did you go to school?) You're still going to have to apply yourself for a solid 2+ hours in front of your computer, but it is doable. (H&R Block took me 1.5 *days*.)

When it's all said and done, I'll spend somewhere around $70 to complete my taxes online with TurboTax. All of the above is by no means a complete guide to paying your taxes, there's much more out there on the subject that I don't know about, but it should at least give you an idea of what you are up against.

Writing a Will

Yeah, nobody likes to think about this stuff. It sucks, but it's part of being an adult. Forget the superstitious crap about how if you write a will you'll die tomorrow. It's superstition and crap.

The truth is unless you want the government to decide who gets all of your stuff and money when you die, you need to have a will written out. Otherwise, when the government decides, they may end up giving your stuff to a relative that you don't really like.

Writing a will is something that you can do yourself. The catch here though is that you aren't a lawyer. You didn't spend years and years studying estate law so that you can craft a loophole-proof will that won't end up with family members squabbling over possessions (it happens).

While I honestly believe that getting a will is more important if you're married, have kids, or actually have some assets, eventually, you are going to reach one of those three variables and you are going to need a will.

What you need to do at that point is to search for estate lawyers within your community. These are the people who write wills for a living. They understand all of the ins and outs of the law in this area, and you are going to want to utilize their expertise.

For me, it took two appointments. The first appointment required discussing with the lawyer what my assets were, who I wanted them to go to, what to do about family stuff, and so on. If I remember correctly, the second appointment was basically just me signing more paperwork and turning more stuff in.

The total cost for me was somewhere around $200 or so as the lawyer gave me a discount since I was young, and writing a young person's will is a cinch compared to an older person worth a million dollars and with a large family.

So, find an estate lawyer in your town that you like and consider getting this done.

FOOD

You have to eat! Like money, food is also going to play a large role in your life multiple times per day. Your food intake is inherently tied to your personal health as well though. Sure, you may think you can save money by eating nothing but potato chips every day, but your health is going to be atrocious.

Whether you're focusing on weight management, fighting food boredom, staying healthy, impressing your date, or just trying to eat food you will enjoy, here is some advice that I believe you'll find you wish school had taught you.

Kitchen Utensils That You Will Need

If you want to cook food, you are going to need a working kitchen. If you want a working kitchen, you are going to need the tools that allow it to actually work. The below list is a basic list that will help you to get things started.

1. **Cutting board** – Because you're going to have to cut things up at just about every meal, and using the countertop can leave it with nasty cut marks all in it.
2. **Knives** – Because karate chopping sometimes just isn't enough.
3. **Serving spoons** – If you want to be able to serve out more than just one bite at a time, you're going to need some serving spoons.
4. **Ladle** – perfect for dishing out soups and chili
5. **Serving dishes** – A great way to ensure everything that you serve isn't in a pot.
6. **Colander** – You need this for straining the water off of different foods that you make.
7. **Mixer** – This allows you to mix ingredients together speedily.
8. **Pots** – To cook stuff on the stove
9. **Oven mitts** –so that you can actually handle what you are working with.
10. **Baking trays** – If you want to make cookies, pizza, bread, or anything else in the oven you are going to

need several of these in various sizes.
11. **Silverware** – You'll actually save yourself a bit of money if you don't constantly have to go and buy plastic spoons and forks.
12. **Plates, bowls, and glasses** – Once again, because buying the disposable stuff gets old real fast.

How to Shop for Groceries

It's weird how something as simple as shopping for food can seem such a daunting proposition. Shopping for groceries? But that's easy you say. Not if you don't want to end up a 600-pound gumdrop.

If you've never had to do it before to survive then there is a bit of a learning curve to it, especially if you don't know how to cook. The first couple of times you do this, you're going to find yourself predominantly buying pre-made convenient stuff. You'll also quickly find that eating this way long-term will make you feel fat, sluggish, and just gross.

That's not sustainable.

You're going to need to learn how to shop in a healthy manner if you want to avoid blowing up like a blimp shortly after you move out to "the real world". So what do you need to know? Well, by following the below bits of advice you'll have a much better understanding of what it takes to eat healthily.

1) **Plan what you are going to make for the week ahead of time** – this allows you to know what ingredients you are going to need. Unless you're an ace in the kitchen, just winging it is going to result in your just eating whatever is quickest and most convenient. Oftentimes this puts us right back to eating crap.

2) **Shop the outside perimeter of the store** – The outside perimeter is predominantly the fresh, non-processed, healthy stuff. If you can do everything you can to avoid the middle of a grocery store you'll be doing pretty good. By buying fresh fruits, veggies, meats, breads, cheeses, yogurts, milks, and juices you'll have the ability to cook virtually anything and you will automatically be eating healthier than if you subsisted on middle of the grocery store stuff.

3) **Coupons and membership discounts rock** – I was never a big couponer until I met my wife. It was then that I realized just how much money you can save over the course of a year by using every discount you can get your hands on for products *you were going to buy anyway* at the grocery store. At this stage of the game, you probably don't have a lot of extra money floating around anyway, so why the heck would you just throw it away?

4) **Take a grocery list** – Research shows that people who actually take a list with them to the grocery store actually end up spending less money than those who don't. Not only does this action help to save your paycheck, but it also ensures that you don't forget anything, that you don't run out of pantry staples, and that you don't end up making impulse purchases as well.

5) **Don't shop hungry** – For real. Eat before you go. Mom always told me this, and I never understood why until I'd gone shopping myself a few times. My grocery bills from when I was hungry were astronomically higher compared to the times I was full when I shopped. I ended

up buying all kinds of things that I didn't need, and later regretted.

Easy-to-Cook Meals

I'm by no means a good cook. I've caught the stove on fire cooking spaghetti, filled the kitchen with smoke baking pizza, and ruined more omelets than you can count. However, learning how to cook is a skill that you are going to need to learn how to do in order to survive on your own. Eating out every meal not only is incredibly expensive but makes it hard to not gain a lot of weight as well.

I don't want to give you a whole bunch of recipes though. There are plenty of other great sources out there for that, and I'm really not that original in the kitchen. Instead, I'm going to point you to several sources that I've found to be incredibly helpful.

1. **The 4-Hour Chef** – I really like Timothy Ferris' books, and this one was great as well. As I've mentioned before, I'm a terrible cook. But reading through this book and experimenting with it not only gave me some semblance of confidence in the kitchen but taught me how to be a bit creative with what I make as well.
2. **Allrecipes.com** – Though I do like having the physical copy of a cookbook to help walk me through what it is I'm making, I don't like having to go out to buy more cookbooks. So instead, I've used this website quite a bit and I think it's great.

3. **Marthastewart.com** – My mom was a huge fan of Martha Stewart while I was growing up, and I can remember seeing cookbooks and recipes from her everywhere. When I moved out on my own, this was one of the sites I regularly would refer to because I knew they would taste good, and be something I could potentially do.
4. **Supercook.com** – I really like this one. Having the forethought to plan out my meals a week or so in advance wasn't ever really a strong suit of mine. Oftentimes I would have a bunch of random ingredients in my pantry and fridge and just didn't know what it was possible to make out of them.

That's where Supercook comes in. With Supercook, you just enter in the ingredients that you do have on their website, and it will spit out a list of potential recipes that you can easily make with what you already have. It's saved me a lot of bland meals and frustration.

Just to give you something of an idea these are some of the meals that I can crank out relatively easily. Yeah, you won't find anything fancy here, but that's the point. For somebody who doesn't have the gift of cooking fantastic food, these are some of the things that can be made without a lot of fuss or strange cooking techniques. I recommend checking them out and then moving on from there.

- Homemade pizza
- Bisquick pancakes/biscuits
- Chili

- Macaroni and cheese
- Grilled cheese
- Paninis
- Bread
- Tacos
- Homemade soup

HEALTH

You live on your own now. You are now an adult. And part of being an adult means you learn what it takes to take care of yourself. You not only should know what this means, but you should know a thing or two about insurance, how to treat the basics, and where to go for help.

How to Navigate Healthcare

Let's delve right into one of the most confusing aspects of health: insurance.

Let's be honest. Navigating healthcare absolutely sucks and can be a constant reminder of the phrase "adding insult to injury". You're already sick or injured, and on top of that, the healthcare system almost tries to leave you as confused, lost, and broke as ever.

Here are the things you need to know.

Always carry your health insurance card with you.

Always. You'll need it whenever you seek a healthcare professional's services. Having your insurance card available means that the insurance you have (which you are paying top dollar for, by the way) will actually be doing its job. In most cases, all you will be required to pay is a token copay, usually $25. The insurance will typically pick up the majority of the tab, and then send you a diminished bill a few days/weeks/months later.

The emergency room is much more expensive than a walk-in clinic or primary health care provider as well.

Going to an ER is going to hurt your wallet severely. Avoid it unless you do actually need an ER. If it's nothing too severe, then a walk-in clinic or primary health care provider (PHCP), your regular doctor, will be a much cheaper way to get the treatment you need.

If you know that you are going to need a prescription medication I highly recommend using goodrx.com prior to having your doctor order your prescription for you.

Goodrx.com allows you to see the prices of the particular medicine you need (and medical services as well) at all of the different doctors and pharmacies in your area. You can often find differences in costs in very large amounts of money. Doing your research first here can save you some serious moolah, especially if you need a particular prescription every month.

If you have to have some type of procedure or operation done, I highly recommend doing a little research with opscost.com first.

The site allows you to compare the prices of common medical procedures across all of the medical facilities in your area. Just playing around with it I've found differences in cost in the thousands of dollars range.

Basic Medicines

In my opinion, one of the worst times to have to go to the store to buy non-prescription medicines is when you actually need them. When you're sick, you don't want to do anything, much less make a trip to Walmart in your PJs.

I quickly learned in college, that keeping a small medicine cabinet filled with some basic medicines made life much more bearable when you feel terrible. Everybody is different, and some people may have allergic reactions or experience strange side effects to different medications, but provided that's not the case I think that the below meds and medical supplies are good to have on hand.

1. **Tylenol** – If you take a hard hit at pickup football, have a headache, or twisted your ankle while hiking. an over the counter medication is a great way to help with pain management. Tylenol blocks the pain receptors in your brain from feeling the signals your body is sending it, and sometimes it can really help to take the edge off with injuries. I always keep at least one bottle at home.
2. **Nyquil** – I tend to buy the off-brand stuff because it's cheaper, but occasionally an illness can make it absolutely miserable to attempt to sleep at night. With Nyquil, you can be out like a light in a few min-

utes, sleep deep through the whole night, and wake up the next morning feeling slightly better (hopefully).

3. **Pepto Bismol** – Trust me, the absolute last time you want to go buy Pepto is when you need it. If you've got indigestion, diarrhea, or the like, you want to be very close to the porcelain throne. This little pink bottle can really help to take the edge off of stomach pain due to both of these situations.

4. **Cough Drops** – If you wake up with a scratchy, sore, miserable throat, then cough drops can help to make it a little more bearable. They come in good flavors too.

5. **Aspirin** – Though in the same boat as ibuprofen, I always keep a small bottle of this handy just in case. If somebody ends up at your place having a heart attack, when you call 911 there's a good chance that the operator will tell you to give the person an aspirin if they're still conscious. Aspirin thins the blood and can make it easier for oxygen to get to strangulated heart tissue in the case of a heart attack.

6. **Neosporin** – If you accidentally cut yourself, Neosporin helps to fight off potential infection.

7. **Hydrogen peroxide** – I use this for the same purposes as Neosporin and then some. Not only does this stuff help to fight off potential infection of a cut, scrape, or another bloody injury, but I also use it to help clean off tweezers, clean popped zits, and the like. It also doubles as mouthwash, but don't swallow it.

8. **Burn gel** – Aloe vera works for this, but some people

are allergic to it. If that's you, they do make burn gel that doesn't contain aloe. Both types will help to ease pain from a burn and help it to heal up quicker.
9. **Tums** – Heartburn is miserable, and it's not fun having to wait an hour going to the store and back to get some relief. These are a nice thing to have on hand perchance you or a guest end up with heartburn while at your place.

These will get you through most of what gets thrown your way. However, I would add a quality first aid kit to the list. Nobody plans on getting injured, but it does happen. When that's the case, it's incredibly frustrating to not have the band-aids, gauze, tweezers, or whatever else that you may need. Most Walmart-esque stores will carry some form of first aid kit, but I've found better-stocked ones for better prices online.

A random note on ibuprofen: a lot of people use ibuprofen as a pain-reliever. If you're a dude, I wouldn't risk it. Recent research from the Proceedings of the National Academy of Sciences has tied ibuprofen use to male sterility. If you want to suffer from erectile dysfunction, reduced testosterone, and risk not being able to have kids in the future, then go ahead. You probably don't though, so find other options.

Emergency Medical Situations

This one's a tricky one. Every situation is different, and it can often be hard to tell the severity of a medical problem without extensive training. What I will say is this though: if you think you need to go to the emergency room, then get there.

I personally wouldn't go there for a little cough or anything like that though. That's what doctor's offices are for. Going to the ER for something minor such as a cold, or a case of the sniffles is only going to result in a gigantic medical bill for something that could have easily been fixed by a walk-in clinic for about 1/10th of the cost.

For your everyday coughs, sniffles, aches, and pains I highly recommend just finding a walk-in clinic somewhere. These places are popping up everywhere and I've had good experiences with the doctors and nurses at every single one. The price is a doctor's price, but it is much more reasonable compared to the bill after bill you are going to get for several months for several different reasons if you decide to visit an emergency room.

What to Do If You Get in a Car Accident

I've been in two car accidents, both fender benders, and they both sucked. A fender bender is normally viewed as a "little" accident. No cars totaled, no lengthy hospital stays. Everything's fine. You'll be ok.

That's how it's viewed anyway. Holy smokes though, did mine ever scare me. For the first one, I was sitting in the left turn lane attempting to turn left. I'd been there for quite a bit of time before an elderly lady slammed into the back of me. I saw her at the last minute, but it was too late. My head hit the window, and I was livid. I immediately called the cops, we both pulled over, and everything ended up being ok.

The second time I was hit, I was sitting at a stoplight. I once again had been there a while when there was a loud bang, and my car screeched forwards. A gigantic work truck had hit me. We both pulled over, but I didn't call the cops, and that's where things went downhill.

The man claimed he had caused no damage to my car, which was clearly false judging by my cracked fender, and smashed in trunk. His buddy in a different work truck also pulled over to back his buddy up. I wasn't hurt, so I figured that all I needed to do was get a signed statement from the guy saying that it was his fault. I thought

I'd be able to just fax this to my insurance company, and they'd give me the money for repairs, and we wouldn't have to involve the cops.

Turns out I should have called the cops.

The jerk said that I slammed on my brakes, and his boss refused to pay for repairs. It ended up with a court date, and me getting the money for the accident that the employer refused to pay me.

If you are ever in an accident, learn from my mistakes. Here is what you should do:

Are you hurt?

If you are hurt, especially around your neck, don't move. Wait for somebody else to call 911. Perchance you have broken your neck, moving could result in paralysis. If it's just mild whiplash, you're probably ok to call 911 yourself. If you're feeling ok, the first thing that you need to do is call 911. Even if you are not hurt, or the damage to your car isn't that bad, call the cops.

The 911 operator will send a cop and potentially an ambulance your way as well.

They're also going to instruct you to get your vehicle out of the road if you can manage to do so. Your ability to move your vehicle will depend on how bad you are hurt, and how bad the damage is to your car. Use your judgment.

If you can do so, you need to gather some information from the other driver.

Get their insurance number, license plate number, name, phone number, and address. Give them yours as well. You'll need this info to make a claim with your insurance company. Without it, you're screwed.

When the police arrive, they will give you a statement saying that you did have an accident, who was at fault, etc.

If you can do so, call your insurance company and begin your claim as soon as possible.

This will ensure that you get the payment you need for car damage, medical expenses, rental car, etc. and in as timely a manner as possible. If you wait several days before calling them they're going to be suspicious about your story and intentions, and that could create a whole host of other issues.

When the cops arrive and say that you are good to go, you can leave if your car is still drivable.

Otherwise, you are going to need to get a tow truck to move your car, and you're probably going to need a taxi or rental car to get to where you need to go as well.

Go to the doctor or hospital if you need to.

As mentioned in step 1, you should always call the cops. Even if it doesn't *look* like there's any damage. Car accidents can often cause hidden damage that will set *you* back thousands of dollars if you do not get the cops to come out and make a statement of who is at fault. In my case, my failure to call the cops cost me close to $500.

My brother was in a fender bender (not his fault) where he just let the guy go, saying that there wasn't any damage. My brother needed a new fender. Guess who paid for it? Not the other guy.

After an accident, you're going to be hopped up on adrenaline. You may not feel any pain. The next day or so after you wake up though things might be a little different. Take it easy for a few days afterward, and go to the doctor if you feel it's wise. If the accident wasn't your fault and you called the cops, the other involved party will pay for the medical expenses, so don't feel that you can't afford to go to the doctor. Especially if you hit your head pretty hard, have a terrible headache, or have pretty bad whiplash, going to see a doctor is important. They can give you stuff to take the edge off of the pain and will ensure that there is not anything worse going on such as a concussion, brain bleed, etc.

Why and How You Should Exercise

You're an adult now. You need to take care of yourself. Otherwise, you will end up sick, injured, or dead.

Part of the equation for health is exercise. You need to make time for it. Not doing so now can result in gaining fat, elevated cholesterol levels that can lead to heart attacks, elevated blood sugar levels that can lead to diabetes, loss of bone mass that can lead to you dying in a nursing home from broken hip complications when you're old, and more.

You *need* to exercise.

Whether you're into running, weight lifting, kayaking, or whatever, you need to make sure that you are doing something and preferably at least 3x/week. Kayaking and backpacking are great sources of exercise, but the chances that you're going to do that 3x/week throughout the course of a year are pretty slim. That's ok if that serves as some of your workouts, but don't rely on the stuff that you can't do consistently.

I'm an exercise physiologist by trade and spent 3 years as a personal trainer as well, so this is something that I'm pretty passionate about. It's when people stop exercising that they grow weak, start to develop aches and pains (even in the absence of injury), end up getting injured badly, lose energy, can't sleep as well anymore, end up stressed out, and often end up depressed as well.

Even if this is something that you don't like, it has to become a part of your weekly routine. Exercise has to be something that you just do without thinking. You want it to get to the point that it is so ingrained in your weekly life that it becomes a habit.

I have a lot that I could say about this, but I'll keep it short and simple. There are a few keys to working out that you need to keep in mind at all times to ensure that you don't get hurt.

Don't do it if it hurts.

Didn't see that coming, did ya? Of course, there's a difference between muscle soreness and actual pain. Muscle soreness happens with exercise. It's expected to an extent. Pain that makes you wince is not. Attempting to push through actual pain only leads to things getting much worse. Use your head. If it hurts, find something else.

It's better to miss a day than to miss a month.

Let me explain this one before you go off believing I'm telling you to skip working out. Some days for whatever reason, your body will just not want to do a particular exercise. It just won't feel right. Something will be overly tight, be kind of inflamed or will just hurt. When that's the case, just skip that one and move on to your other exercises. I've found that pushing through these weird pains only results in you actually ending up injured and having to miss a month of that exercise just so that you can heal up.

It's better to just skip that one for the day and come back to it fully functioning on your next workout.

Check your ego at the door.

Part of the fun of working out is being able to push yourself to your limits. I understand that. But it's when your ego gets in the way that you end up making really stupid decisions that will only serve to get you hurt. When you try to show off in front of a girl or try to prove to the guys that you can bench the extra 15 pounds than your known max you're just setting yourself up for trouble. Check your ego at the door. Your body will thank you.

What to Do if You Get Pregnant

Nobody prepares you for parenthood. It kind of just slaps you in the face, I've been told. If you're married and have been actively planning a pregnancy that's one thing. But what do you do when you aren't and never had any intention of this happening to *you*?

If you aren't ready to be a parent, there are plenty of infertile couples out there who would absolutely love to adopt your little baby.

The first thing that I would do would be to get online and find the nearest pregnancy help center near you.

They will help to walk you through all of the necessary steps throughout the entire 40 weeks of your pregnancy. Many of these are attached to local churches in your area, and churches are filled with loving, generous people. They will help to ensure that you are taken care of in whatever way that you need to be throughout this journey.

If you're married and you end up pregnant checking into a pregnancy help center isn't for you. You need to move on to step 2.

Your first step is going to have to go to the doctor.

Schedule an appointment with yours, or even just go into a walk-in clinic to get an appointment. This will get the ball rolling medically to help keep you on track with all of the medical stuff that you're going to have to get straightened out. They can help you with nausea, will give you advice, and will schedule your ultrasounds to see how the baby is doing.

Taking prenatal vitamins may be a good idea as well.

These tend to be high in folic acid, something that decreases the risk of the baby being born with neural tube defects. You want to make sure that both you and the baby are getting the proper nutrition.

Avoid alcohol and tobacco as well.

Using either of these substances throughout the course of a pregnancy can lead to a baby that is born with serious birth defects. Fetal alcohol syndrome is very real, and I can't imagine the pain that comes with knowing that you personally are responsible for the impaired life that your child will have with their time on earth.

SAFETY

Intrinsically tied with your health is your safety. Nobody wants to be an idiot, but sometimes we don't realize we were so until well after the fact. Experience makes for a great (and often brutal) teacher. The wise man learns from the mistakes of others, however, and so, let's see if there aren't some lessons on general safety you wish school had taught you.

General Safety

An ounce of prevention is worth a pound of cure. I remember reading that when I was a little kid, and it just really stuck with me for some reason. All through both college and grad school, I saw instance after instance in the scientific literature which proved just how much this simple statement was true.

When it comes to your own safety, this proverb still stands. Criminals prefer easy prey. If you're going to rob somebody, it works a whole lot better if you're confident you'll be successful.

Lock your doors and windows

If you're going to leave your house, don't make it easy for a bad guy to get your stuff. The same goes for your car. A locked door can not only serve as a preventative ("well, I guess we'll try another."), but it can also buy you some time.

It takes time to pick through a lock, and noise to break through the glass. Either one of these can result in the bad guy getting caught. Even if you're at home I recommend locking your doors. If somebody does try to break in while you're there at least you'll have a little bit of time to call 911, hide, or prepare to fight.

Be aware of your surroundings

It's the people that keep their heads on a swivel that know what is going on around them. If you constantly walk to class, the store, or home with your nose buried in your phone not only are you much more likely to be a target but you could get hurt in an accident as well.

Stepping in potholes, off of steps, into traffic, and into other dangerous situations have all happened as a result of people not paying attention to what is going on around them. I work with patients every day who have been injured as a result of not being vigilant.

If you're going way out, tell people where you're going and what time they can expect you back

I like to hike. I like to take road trips by myself. But I've also read enough of the news to know that bad things can happen to you when you end up stuck somewhere without anybody else in the world having a clue where you are at, or that you're even gone to begin with. (Anybody else out there read *Between a Rock and a Hard Place*? The guy didn't tell people where he was going, got his arm trapped while bouldering in the middle of nowhere, and had to cut it off with a dull knife several days later to get out of there)

It doesn't take a long time to send a quick group message to two friends you trust telling them where you are going and for approximately how long. The 10 seconds it takes to do this could easily be what saves your life.

Don't travel in dangerous areas

Yeah, this one seems like a given, but I'm constantly surprised by the number of people that do this unwittingly. What's worse, nobody seems to think that they do travel in dangerous areas when you confront them about it.

If where you're at regularly appears in Robert Pelton's *The World's Most Dangerous Places* then you need to find someplace else to be.

There's a part of town where I live where people get shot, beat up, and mugged on a daily basis. Gangs rule there, and the cops only show up when they can show up in force. Despite this, a friend of my wife decided to park in this area and walk a mile or so to the safe part of downtown for a festival.

It was close to 10 PM when she decided she was going to start walking back. Uhhh, no. That's stupid. We gave her a ride and told her about the area. She had no clue. Typically you'll have some shred of sense with where you're at. If you don't want to get blown up, don't walk through the minefield. Yeah, you could still step on a mine somewhere else, but your odds of making it are much better than they would be in the minefield.

Keep a fire extinguisher in your house

If there is a fire at your place, having a fire extinguisher handy can literally save your home. I've had friends who would have likely lost their entire place had they not been able to extinguish the fire in their kitchen. Having one may lower your renter's insurance rates as well.

Know some basic self-defense moves

The viewing of martial arts as something only nerds do is a recent phenomenon. All throughout human history people knew how to fight. Their lives depended on it. 400 years ago men's men knew how to fight with knives. Now if somebody trains with a knife they're viewed as a weirdo.

You're gonna have to get past this stereotype if you want to be able to better protect yourself and those you love. At the very least I'd say you should learn how to block a punch, how to get out of a headlock, and how to hit somebody fast and hard. Take a class somewhere if you can. If that's not an option for you, I highly recommend watching Master Wong's Wing Chun Tai Chi channel on YouTube. He has some of the most practical videos out there that I've seen such as how to get out of a headlock, how to fight a taller opponent, how to block a kick, etc.

Wear a seat belt

This should be common sense by now, ya'll. Don't end up being a vegetable for the rest of your life because you were in "too much of a hurry" to wear a seatbelt. Show some common sense. Many states actually have laws now against wearing seat belts as well. Where I live, not wearing a seat belt is a reason for a cop to pull you over and give you a ticket. You don't want that. Wear your seat belt.

Don't text and drive

When I first turned 16 my Dad gave me a binder that he had been compiling for who knows how long with nothing but newspaper clippings of teenagers who had died in car accidents. What a gift.

It was a weird way for a parent to show their love, but it was because he didn't want me to end up in some other strange father's death-by-car portfolio. As I read through the stories, over and over I read about how the driver had been toying with their phone.

Even if you don't end up a statistic, is it really worth the spike your insurance rates will see if you rear-end somebody else at a light? And even if it's not you that dies, if you end up hitting a pedestrian with a stroller and killing their kid, you're going to spend a looooong time locked away behind bars (as you should be).

Put the dang phone away.

Keep a knife in your car within reach

I always have a knife on me. I guess it was just part of how I grew up. But it wasn't until my uncle told me this story that I got my wife to carry a knife in her car 24/7 as well.

His car started smoking, so he pulled over to the side of the road. As soon as he did, the car burst into flames. There was an oil leak in his engine that had burst into flames. As the fire grew, he attempted to unlock his seatbelt, but for some reason, it had locked. He never figured out if it was some type of lock attached to the car's computer or what.

Either way, he was trapped. The flames grew to engulf the car, and he still couldn't unlock his seatbelt. That's when he found the box cutter he had in his door's side pocket and used it to cut himself out from the belt. If it hadn't been for having a knife handy, he would have burned to death in his car.

Though you may not end up trapped within a burning car (and no, this isn't a reason to not wear a seat belt), you'd be surprised at just how handy keeping a knife around is.

Keep a breakdown kit in your car

Nobody plans on their car breaking down. Regardless, it happens. And when it does you're going to be miles from help, running late for a smoking hot first date, and you'll have to poop. And it's raining.

With a few basic tools, you can make breakdowns much less spartan. For starters, I'd say to buy yourself a T-bar tire iron and throw it in your trunk. It'll make changing tires infinitely easier than using the puny piece of metal that your car comes with.

A blanket can also make being stuck much more bearable (and safe) if it is particularly cold outside and your car won't start. Imagine being broken down on the side of the road in the middle of December in Vermont while you're in shorts on the way to the gym. A blanket can make that 45 minutes before somebody gets there to help you a whole lot more bearable.

Lastly, I'd recommend a flashlight. Changing tires at night is much easier if you can actually see what is going on. It's also much easier to flag down potential help if they can see you.

Aside from those three things, I'd also recommend:

- Gloves
- Water bottle
- Energy bar
- Lighter
- Screwdrivers
- Wrenches
- Duct tape
- First aid kit
- Walmart bags
- Tire pressure gauge
- One can of Fix-A-Flat

All of the above-bulleted points can easily fit inside a small Tupperware box that you leave in your trunk. Once you set it up, you can pretty much forget it, and you'll have it there for when you eventually need it.

Don't walk or run at night.

I think this one mainly depends on where you live and what your gender is, but as a whole, I still don't recommend it. If you live in a safer area, this may be ok. If you're a dude rather than an attractive lady who looks like an easy target, then this may be ok. If you don't live down an old country road, this may be ok.

But even if none of those above situations apply to you directly, bad stuff has still happened to people in places that nobody would have ever thought it could. Just keep your head about you when you're making these types of decisions.

What to Do if You Get Mugged

Imagine you just finished hanging out with some of your friends at a really great coffee shop downtown late on a Saturday night. You're walking back to your car alone when a man in a black hoodie steps out from behind an alley and demands that you give him your wallet, keys, and phone.

What do you do in a situation like this?

I'll start off by saying that getting mugged is an entirely individualized experience. Sorry, but there's no cookie cutter recipe here to follow. What I can give you are a few general guidelines to follow.

If all the person wants is materialistic (e.g. money, keys, phone), I'd say just go ahead and give it to them. That new smartphone is in no way worth your life or well-being. The bad guy probably has a weapon, and even if they don't kill you with it, is it really worth ending up paralyzed or getting your leg amputated because the bad guy stabbed a blood vessel?

Nope, I don't think so.

Even if the bad guy doesn't show a weapon, that doesn't mean that they don't have one. And even if they really *don't* have one, that doesn't mean that they lack the skills to beat your face so bad that you wake up needing a plastic surgeon.

According to the FBI in 2010, 41.4% of robberies involve firearms, 42.0% involve physical force, 7.9% involved knives or other sharp objects, and 8.8% involved other dangerous weapons.[1]

So if they want materials, I'd just give whatever they wanted to them. You can always buy another phone. You can't buy a new spinal cord or eyeball.

Let's say that the bad guy or bad guys don't want just possessions though. Let's say that they have a darker intent in mind and they're trying to either rape, kidnap, beat, or kill you. In that case, I'd say let them experience your full anger. Fight like your life depends on it because in that case it probably does.

The odds of surviving a kidnapping are incredibly slim, and you don't know what exactly is going to happen to you if they do manage to get you in the trunk of a car. Getting sold into prostitution, being locked up in a basement and repeatedly raped, or being hacked apart are just a few of the many end scenarios that have happened to people that were kidnapped before.

If this is the case, fight hard, *scream* loud (I've always thought it would be a good idea to scream the word "Rape". Even if that's not what's happening, it's vile enough of a crime that it'll get a Good Samaritan's attention and hopefully get you out of the situation), and fight nasty. Anything goes here. Use whatever weapon you can, and do not hold back, because I guarantee you that the bad guy won't. Once you've subdued them, run as fast as you can to help and get the cops over there as quickly as you can.

Obviously, the best thing to do is to avoid getting mugged in the first place. Keep your head on a swivel at all times. Know what is going on around you. Muggers like to target people that are unaware of their surroundings.

I had an intern once who showed up to work with a black eye. Turns out he had been grocery shopping in a very bad part of town. He was exiting the store walking to his car and the next thing he knows, he's waking up in the parking lot with no wallet and no phone. Someone had snuck up to him and sucker punched him. You have to be aware of your surroundings.

Stay away from stupidly dangerous areas too. You're smart enough to know where the bad parts of town are. Avoid them if you can. Try to avoid walking around places at night. If you are going to walk around at night, take a buddy. An extra friend is not only a deterrent but is a potential ally as well should things turn into a brawl.

I'll leave you with this story. A female friend of mine who is about 5'5" tall and weighs *maybe* 110 pounds was traveling alone through the middle of nowhere on her way home from college. She'd drank a lot of water and really had to pee, so she stopped at the only convenience store around for miles. No nearby houses, no nearby shops, just this convenience store. As she walked in she said asked the cashier, a gruff-looking man where the restrooms were.

He pointed out the way and she walked on in. As she was in the stall, she heard the bathroom door open, and steps coming towards her stall. A pair of big brown work boots stopped right in front of her stall facing her door. She pretended she was on the phone with her dad, saying something to the effect of "Yeah Dad, I'm just 2 minutes ahead of you at the gas station. I'll meet you here in a few."

At this, the boots turned around and quickly left. She booked it out of the gas station, but on the way out caught a glimpse of the cashier wearing the exact same big brown work boots that had been at her stall. Nobody else was in the convenience store.

Use your head. Keep aware of your surroundings. Know when to fight. Fight without mercy when you have to.

What are Your Rights When Interacting with Police

There's been a lot of negative press on the police force over the last few years on TV. It's too bad, really. I fully support our police officers and appreciate their putting their lives on the line for law and order on a daily basis. However, I've seen enough of these stories to understand that people seem to be oblivious to what you should do if the police approach you. I by no means am a legal expert, and you may want to consult your individual state laws on the subject, but as a rule of thumb, here are your rights when being confronted by the police:

1. You have the right to remain silent. Just tell the cop that is what right you are exercising before you do it.
2. You have the right to refuse to a search of yourself, your car, or your home. Until they come with a warrant that is. When they have a warrant, you have to let them search. A cop still has the right to pat you down for a weapon though. If police believe your car contains evidence of a crime then they don't need your consent to search it.
3. If you are not under arrest, you have the right to calmly leave.
4. If arrested, you have the right to speak with a lawyer, and should ask for one immediately.
5. Show him your ID if he asks to see it

6. Take the breathalyzer if he asks you to do so or your driver's license will be automatically suspended.

Regardless of whether you are in the right or wrong, for every police encounter please do the following as well:

1. Be polite and courteous
2. Do not lie or give false information
3. Keep your hands visible at all times
4. Don't make sudden movements
5. Do not touch them
6. Do not run.
7. Do not resist arrest if they choose to arrest you.
8. Ask if you are under arrest, because if you are not, then you can leave.

If you don't follow the last 8 points you could make your life infinitely worse, and potentially shorter as well. If you want to avoid being shot, harassed, arrested, or put into prison just swallow your pride, and be as respectful as you can to somebody who you may not feel like being respectful to at all.

Self-Defense

If you're legally allowed, I highly recommend buying a gun for your house to use in self-defense. Even if you don't like the idea of a gun being in your house, you may quickly change your mind when you realize somebody you don't know is peeking through your bedroom door at 3 AM.

If you get a gun, learn how to use it though. Otherwise, all you have is an expensive stick. Learn how to use your gun, and treat it with respect. It can kill somebody. It's not something you just want to be throwing around and dropping everywhere. Accidental discharges of firearms can take you out (it caused my buddy to almost lose his hand).

So if you can get yourself a weapon, do it. Take a firearms safety course, become familiar with how your weapon works, and keep it in a safe place where small children aren't going to find it. You also want to keep it readily available if you need to. 3 AM when someone is trying to break through your bedroom door is a bad time to need the gun that's locked up in a case in the back of the closet in the living room.

I also think you should learn some basic unarmed self-defense as well. Knowing how to punch and kick correctly, knowing opponents' weak spots, how to get out of a headlock, how to block a punch – all of these are very practical skills that could literally save your life someday.

There are a lot of great sources out there for this kind of stuff. A simple Google search will likely reveal half a dozen different martial arts classes in your area. YouTube can even teach you stuff here. My favorite YouTuber on the subject is Master Wong.

HOME

You'll quickly find that home is where you'll pour most of your money, where you'll spend most of your time, and (potentially) where you'll want to get the chance to actually rest in. Oftentimes, it seems as if you pay for a place you never get to use since you're always working.

Here are some of the basics of making your very own home you'll wish school had taught you.

How to Shop for an Apartment

Shopping for a place to live in my opinion is one of the most frustrating things about just starting out. It's about as stressful as it gets. What can I afford? Am I going to be living in a dump? Are the neighbors criminals? These were just a few of the questions I had the first couple of times I moved around and you probably will too.

To start with you do need to figure out a price range.

What *can* you really afford to be paying per month in rent? What are you willing to pay each month for rent as well? Yeah, you may be able to afford to pay $900/month for that ritzy apartment with the bidet, but do you really want to? That's a question you're going to have to answer as well and is going to be really individualized.

Grab a couple of the apartment finder magazines next time you go out to eat, and search online. I've found Zillow, Apartment Finder, and Hot Pads to all do a great job of giving you a pretty comprehensive idea of what's on the market in your area. You'll be able to filter your specifications to what you need as well, so you don't have to sift through pages of mansions.

What do you need in an apartment?

How much space do you need? Do you need one bathroom or do you need two? If you have guests over a lot or do a lot of entertaining, two is probably best (or 1`.5. A half bathroom is one that's just a toilet and a sink. No shower or tub.) If you have a pet, you're going to need to make sure that the apartment is pet-friendly.

How much storage do you need? Is there plenty of closet space available? Is the kitchen big enough to make being there something that you won't dread? Are there hookups for the washer and dryer? If not, you're going to have to do your laundry at a laundromat, and that can get very expensive very quickly.

Has the landlord had a pest problem?

This is something that I would have never thought to ask about. But then we moved into a townhouse and found bedbugs there within the first week. I'd never even thought about asking the landlord if those had previously been a problem. If the landlord ever has had any type of pest problem, keep looking elsewhere.

Where to look for an apartment?

Knowing where to look can sometimes be half the battle. Here are my three top sites for looking for apartments.

- **Zillow.com** – This is the gold standard, and is easily the most popular real estate site out there. If the apartment you're looking for isn't on Zillow, the landlord is clueless. There are plenty of filters on this site to find what you're looking for, and the map drawing ability is pretty nifty too.
- **Hotpads** – I always make sure to check Hotpads as

well. Though not as popular as Zillow, you don't have to sort through as much junk oftentimes. The apartments have different pins on the map depending on what type of housing it is as well. This can make sorting through all those spots on the map much simpler.
- **Apartmentfinder.com** – I save this one for last. Every once in a while you'll find something here that hasn't been posted on the other sites, but Zillow is still my go-to.

Basic Tools You Should Have

Every adult should have a few basic tools around the house. You need to be able to fix things in a timely manner, keep problems from becoming worse, and hang pictures. You don't need to buy every other tool that you see on the shelf at Home Depot nor should you, but a basic tool collection will make your life much easier on your own.

If you're on a budget, I'd strongly recommend looking for these items at garage sales, flea markets, or discount tool stores like Harbor Freight. You can find some awesome deals at these places in my experience.

Here's what I recommend to start:

A good screwdriver set – You'd be surprised by the number of times you are going to need a screwdriver. You can get a good set with 10+ screwdrivers of various lengths, sizes, and head types (flat/Phillips/etc.) for around $15.

A claw hammer – You're going to need to be able to pull nails and *gasp* hammer them as well so make sure you get yourself a good claw hammer. You don't need anything fancy, and bigger doesn't always equal better here. Just get yourself one with a nice wooden handle for around $10-15.

A tape measurer – As a little kid, I grew up watching my dad clip one of these things to his hip just about every morning. He would use it to measure, I would use it to poke people. Next to a screwdriver, a tape measurer is probably going to be the tool that you use most. If you need to move furniture, hang pictures, build something, or who knows what else you're going to need a good quality tape measurer.

As far as length goes, you can probably get by with a 25' tape. At this stage in the game, anything larger is most likely going to be overkill.

A decent quality power drill – I use my drill just about every other day. There's always something that needs to be fixed, something I want to make, or something that I want to install where a drill is needed. There are dozens of different varieties on the market with brands such as DeWalt, Ryobi, Milwaukee, Black and Decker, and Craftsman.

This is an area where I don't like to skimp. My dad and papa always taught me to buy the best grade tools that I could at the price that I could afford because if you did they would last you for the rest of your life. Now a power drill is most definitely not gonna last you the rest of your life, but a good quality one will make using it much more enjoyable.

When I first started out on my own, I bought a Black and Decker power drill for around $40. I got what I paid for. It worked fine for a lot of the little things that I needed to do around the house, but when my friend asked me to help him hang his new TV on the wall we quickly found out that my little drill didn't have the power needed to drill through a stud in the wall. I went out and got a Milwaukee soon after.

Do a little research here first and find out what you like. Ryobi and Black and Decker have a reputation for being cheap in more ways than one. Some people use nothing but these brands and crank out fantastic projects. I'd say they're the exception to the rule though. DeWalt and Milwaukee are decent brands in my book, and can take heavy use for a much longer time. . They'll probably set you back around $100, but the money is well worth it.

Pliers – Sometimes things get stuck, and a good pair of pliers will help you to get them unstuck. Gripping torn-out screws, tightening nuts and bolts, and crimping wires are just a few of the things that you'll use pliers for.

You can get a good pair for less than $7, or you can typically find a set with a bunch of different types for around $15-$20.

Adjustable wrenches – Adjustable wrenches can really help you to tackle a wide range of nut, screw, and bolt sizes. All you have to do is adjust the scroller wheel with your thumb until the wrench has a good grip on whatever it is that you need to tighten/loosen. I'd recommend getting a small set of these with varying handle lengths. You should be able to get them for around $15.

A bullet level – This is a little level about 6" long that will help to ensure that you're not hanging pictures all throughout your house so that it looks like you just got hit by an earthquake. You can pick this up for around $5, and you'll use it a lot.

A stud finder – You're going to want to hang pictures in your house, and if they have any heft to them whatsoever, you're probably going to want to find a stud to put your nails/screws into. It's really hard to do that without a stud finder. You can pick these up for around $20, but I recommend getting one that also lets you know if you're anywhere near a hot wire. Being shocked via a nail isn't fun when you're attempting to balance on the back of your couch to get that family portrait just perfect.

A toolbox – You're going to need a place to put all of these tools, and they don't look good in a little pile in the corner of your bedroom, so I recommend getting a good toolbox. I use a rusty, beat-up old thing that my dad gave me that works fine. You don't need anything fancy here. You just want something sturdy enough to hold what you need without spilling tools all over the floor. A 5-gallon plastic bucket is cheap and works great for this.

A square – This looks like a triangle with ruler markings on it, and if you build anything you will use it for just about every project. A square allows you to calculate angles, and get a perfect 90-degree cut. Without a square, you'll have an almost impossible time being able to get the right angle for your cut, and then you'll just end up ruining a board and wasting money. Harbor Freight has these for around $5.

As time goes on and new projects come up, you're definitely going to want to add to this list, but this list will pretty much get you through the majority of what gets thrown your way for a little while.

How to Clean a House

You don't realize how many people don't know how to do this until you have roommates. Unless you want your friends to dread coming over to your place because of the science project growing in the toilet, you need to regularly clean your house. Dishes are something that we do every day at my place. Laundry is done every week as is cleaning floors, vacuuming, dusting, taking the trash out, and the like.

A clean house will help to keep you healthy as well. I do understand the confusion that comes when you look at the cleaning products aisle at Walmart though and wonder just what cleaner can you use without melting a hole through your countertops. Thankfully, a little bit of know-how and experience goes a long way here.

Need to clean windows or other pieces of glass?

I use Windex for everything glass. It does a fantastic job. All you need here is the Windex and a paper towel or some type of rag. Squirt the Windex on and immediately start cleaning it off with the paper towel. I wipe it off in small overlapping circles until there are no more streaks or dirty spots anywhere.

Need to clean a toilet?

Cleaning a toilet is probably the most intimidating part

of a house to clean. *But I go POOP in there!* Yeah, yeah. We know. They're pretty easy to clean though.

Pour some Clorox in the bowl, let it sit for a while, and then scrub down the insides with a toilet brush before flushing it all down the drain. For the outside of the toilet, I use some type of cleaner that's safe to use on porcelain and wipe it all down with paper towels. I don't like using a sponge on the toilet because then you have to find a place to store the poo-poo sponge. Paper towels are disposable, and have won my heart on the matter.

I use gloves when cleaning a toilet as well. You'd be surprised how many people don't. I don't like touching toilet brushes with my bare hands, don't really like touching toilets with my bare hands, but most importantly I don't like touching those cleaning products with my bare hands. A lot of those cleaning products can be absorbed through your skin doing who knows what to your insides.

A friend of a friend ended up destroying his body's ability to produce testosterone by regularly spraying weed killer while wearing flip-flops. The stuff got on his toes and into his body. I know cleaning agents aren't weed killers, but who's to say they couldn't do similar things to your hormones? Play it safe. Wear gloves.

Need to clean a floor?

This is going to depend on what type of floor you're cleaning. Is it wood, tile, laminate, or something else? Each type is going to need a different type of cleaner or you risk ruining the floor. We have laminate throughout the kitchen and living room at our house. I typically use a Swiffer wet mop. The pads are disposable, they do a good job of cleaning up the floor, and I don't have to store an actual nasty mop anywhere.

If there's something on the floor that my Swiffer won't get up (which is rare), then I usually have to get down onto my hands and knees and scrub whatever it is up with soap and a sponge. As long as you clean up messes before they dry though you should be able to avoid this.

Need to clean a carpet?

Vacuuming is going to be the main thing that you do to clean a carpet. If the carpet has stains all over it and is a mess, then it may be worth actually steam cleaning the thing. You can hire somebody out to do this, but it's cheaper to rent one yourself. Walmart rents them out as do other places. You run the thing just like you would a vacuum and it ensures that your carpet is getting a deep clean.

If there are just a few stains here and there I use a spot remover. Spot Shot is the one I use the most often, as I feel it does a good job without discoloring my carpet. Just follow the directions on the can of whatever you get, and you should be able to get out most stains.

For stains made by a pet, you can get special cleaners that are specifically made for carpet that's been pooped or peed on. They work, but I've never been 100% happy with them, and some of them stain in my experience.

Your best bet is to just keep Fido from crapping in your house.

Need to clean a countertop or tabletop?

Both of these areas are incredibly important to keep clean. Your food and kitchen utensils will come into contact with these surfaces, and if you do not keep them as clean as you can, you could end up seriously sick. What happens if your roommate makes a sandwich right where you were cutting raw chicken earlier? They could end up in a hospital potentially thanks to your salmonella.

I use soap and water with a rag first. That allows me to scrub up any junk that's hardened somewhere. Afterward, I spray the counter/table down with some Lysol and wipe it up with a paper towel. That way I know I've not only removed all of the crud, but I've killed all of the germs as well.

Need to clean a sink or a bathtub?

Most likely you'll be able to use the same cleaner that you used to clean the outside of your toilet bowl. Squirt the stuff around the surface that you need to clean and then get to scrubbing with a sponge. The sinks don't tend to be as bad, but cleaning the bathtub can take a bit of time just because of how big they are. Have fun in there!

How to Patch a Hole in Drywall

Your nerf basketball game got a little too intense, huh? How you patch a hole in drywall will really depend on the size of the hole. For little stuff, all you'll need is spackle, a scraper, and sandpaper.

You put the spackle in the hole, scrape it flat with the scraper, and then let it dry. After the spackle has dried thoroughly you're going to want to sand the spackle smooth. This will help the hole to disappear when you paint back over it.

If you don't sand the spackle smooth you're going to end up with this nasty-looking blemish on your wall after you paint it that screams to all of your friends that you have absolutely no idea what you're doing.

For bigger holes, you're going to need drywall mesh. Drywall mesh is a fine metal screen that you'll want to cut to a size slightly larger than the hole you are filling. The mesh gives the spackle something to stick to. Spackle everything over and then gently scrape it as smooth as possible without pushing the mesh in.

Sand everything smooth after it's dried, and voila, you're done.

How to Use a Plunger

Once upon a time, a friend of mine invited a bunch of us over to her house. We hung around and ate quite a bit of guacamole. She soon after excused herself to the restroom. When she returned she sheepishly looked at me and asked me if I knew how to use a plunger.

Talk about taking your friendship to the next level.

You don't want to be that person. You don't want to be the friend that has to ask somebody at a party to unclog the toilet packed with your dookie. You need to know how to use a plunger.

So, should the toilet ever refuse to flush for you here is how to use a plunger.

1. Place the plunger suction cup (please not the stick) into the toilet slowly so it doesn't splash (you'll only make this mistake once).
2. Place the plunger suction cup over the hole in the bottom of the toilet and slowly push against it until the plunger collapses in on itself. Again you want to do this slowly so that you don't splash crap all over your khakis. That's also going to be the only time this happens to you. When you're wearing nice clothes.
3. Slowly release the plunger so that it goes back to its normal shape and press again. Repeat this until the

water has been plunged out of the toilet.
4. Hopefully, by this point, the clog has been pushed past where it was stuck and the toilet has automatically flushed itself and refilled. If that is not the case, go ahead and flush again to get the toilet to fill up with water again. Keep plunging away until the clog is fixed.

How to Hang a Picture

If you don't know how to hang a picture properly, one of two things will happen. Either your house will look like it was decorated by a kindergartener with a hammer, or it will be barren, giving a distinctive prison vibe.

Neither of these options really appeals to me (nor my wife), and they probably don't appeal to you either. So, we need to learn how to hang a picture.

Exactly how you hang a picture on your walls really depends on the size and weight of the picture. Most pictures tend to be pretty light. These can typically be hung in drywall with a simple nail without any problem. If you try to hang something heavy with a single nail in drywall though, you may wake up one night to a loud crash, only to find that there is broken glass on your floor and a chunk missing from your wall.

So weight is going to really determine what goes on here. If we're trying to hang something heavier on a wall, putting the nails/screws into a stud is generally a good idea. The stud is the 2×4 board behind the drywall that forms part of the framing of the wall. It's secured into place pretty strongly and can support a good deal of weight. As a result, if you place screws or nails into these, the odds that your picture is going to pull itself off of the wall are slim to none.

What do you do if the picture you want to hang is really heavy and there aren't any studs around where you want to hang it though? Or what do you do if the picture is really long, and you only have a stud on one of the sides? How do you hang it then?

In both of these cases, you're going to want to use something known as a drywall anchor. You can pick small packages of these up at hardware stores for a couple of bucks, and it's basically a plastic screw with a metal screw that goes into it. As the metal screw screws into the plastic screw, the very tip of the plastic screw will separate and expand in two different directions 'anchoring' it into place. This expansion makes it incredibly difficult for the drywall anchor to be pulled out of the wall via gravity.

You also want to make sure that you don't drive a screw or a nail into a wire. Doing so can short out the wire leading to much bigger problems. To avoid this I highly recommend buying a stud finder that will also tell you if there is a hot wire anywhere nearby. Typically, these stud finders will have a special flashing light that lets you know if they are anywhere near electricity. This allows you to find a safer spot to put your nails/screws instead.

Knowing all of this, let's go over how to hang a picture nice and level.

1. Find the points(s) where you are going to insert your nail(s) or screw(s). If you only need to install one, put it in, hang your picture, use a bullet level to make it level, and voila! You're finished.

2. If you need to insert multiple nails or screws, find the points that you want to insert them, and make sure that they are all level with each other. If the points are not level with each other, then the picture isn't going to be level either. I use a tape measure or a long level to help me figure out this.
3. Once the points are level, insert your screws, nails, or drywall anchors.
4. Hang your picture on whatever you just put into the wall.
5. Use a level to make any fine-tuning adjustments, if need be.

This method will help you hang the majority of pictures out there without any problems.

If you've got a bit of extra cash, there is a tool out there that will make this whole process infinitely easier. There are stud finders out there that have a built-in laser level in them. All you do is put the stud finder on the wall and press the laser button. This will send a laser line all the way across the wall in both directions, and it will automatically level itself.

It's not cheap, but it'll definitely help you to hang things faster and with less hassle.

What to Do with a Clogged Sink

Regardless of how clean you keep your kitchen/bathroom, eventually, you will have a sink clog. I'm about 97% positive it's going to happen to you when you're in a hurry. So what can you do to fix the issue? I follow these three steps:

1) **Use a drain stick.**

This is an incredibly handy tool that looks like a long plastic strip with spikes all down each side. They cost about $5 or so and you can find them readily in the plumbing section of any hardware store. The one I buy is called a Cobra and I get it at Lowe's. All you have to do is shove the drain stick down the clogged pipe, and then pull it on up.

I'll give you fair warning on this one though. Put your sunglasses on first, and don't be wearing nice clothes at the time either because there is a good chance that you're going to get splattered with some funk. The little spikes on the drain stick will grab onto any trapped debris that is stuck down in your drain (especially hair) and then pull back a slimy, boogery, hairball mess.

It's disgusting, but it's one of those things you quickly yell for everybody in the whole house to come and look at.

2) **If the drain stick doesn't work (and sometimes it**

won't) then I often resort to using Drain-O or some similar type of pipe cleaning liquid.

This usually means that the clog is much deeper than the stick can reach, or is comprised of an unknown substance that the drain stick can't grab.

When using these chemicals be incredibly careful. I always make sure that I'm wearing gloves and protective glasses. They are incredibly strong acids and if they get on you they can jack you up. So be careful with them. Follow the directions on the bottle to a tee, and check back soon afterward to see if your drain is still clogged or not. Hopefully, by this point, you've solved the problem.

If neither of those two methods works, there's the chance that you have something bigger stuck on down there that the acid couldn't dissolve. Maybe something is trapped in the little U-shaped pipe under the sink. That tends to be an easy place for stuff to get stuck. I personally check that next which involves taking pipes apart, a process I'm not going to tell you about here.

If you don't feel comfortable removing pipes or if there's still nothing trapped in the U pipe under the sink you may have to call a plumber to fix the issue as it could be further down the pipes farther than you can hit.

Lawnmower stuff

Moving into your own place may mean that you need to finally take care of *your own* lawn. You can either pay a landscaper to mow your lawn for you, or you can do it yourself. It has to be done. Just leaving it be will make your neighbors hate you, and in some cases can get you fined if the homeowner's association has some type of policy regarding grass height.

You have to mow your grass. Finding somebody to do it for you is as easy as a quick Google search. Craigslist might be worth your time as well. There's the potential to find younger guys just starting out there who may not charge as much as the professionals.

If you choose to do it yourself though you are going to need a lawnmower and a weed eater.

There are two types of lawnmower: riding and push. A riding mower is what you sit and ride on. It's good if you have a whole lot of grass to cut. A push mower has to be pushed by you. A push mower is most likely what you need at this stage in the game. Not only are they much cheaper than riding lawnmowers, but they also are easier/cheaper to fix, easier to store, and in my opinion don't have as many issues to begin with.

You can always get a new one at Lowe's or Home Depot, but I've had good experiences with used ones as well.

Craigslist, yard sales, and newspaper classifieds are all good alternatives for finding a quality used push mower.

You're going to need a weed eater as well. Without it you have no way of getting the tall grass off the edges of fences, walls, retaining walls, etc. You need a weed eater. How much you pay is going to depend on how much you need to mow. If you have acres of grass, it may be worth your time to get a higher-quality weed eater. If not, something cheaper should do.

You're going to need fuel for your grass mowing equipment as well. Every riding mower I've ever used has taken just straight-up gasoline. I've never had to add anything or buy special gas or anything like that. There may be exceptions out there, but none that I'm aware of.

Weed eaters are trickier. Weed eaters need the addition of engine oil to the gasoline or else the fuel will clog the fuel filter or cause your engine to become virtually worthless. My current weed eater takes what's called 2-cycle engine oil. It comes in a teeny little bottle from Lowe's near the lawn care equipment. I add one entire bottle to one gallon of gasoline. Then it's safe for my weed eater to use.

Different weed eaters may need different types of engine oil. Ask the previous owner or consult the instruction manual to figure out what type you need. The important thing to remember is that you always treat your weed eater gasoline with engine oil. Otherwise, you'll end up buying another weed eater real quick.

Household Items You Will Need

There's more to having your own place than paying the electric bill and keeping food in the fridge. There are a number of items that your home is going to need if you don't want it to end up being run-down, butt-nasty, and not a relaxing environment. The below list will help to get you started.

1) **Vacuum** – If you have carpeting where you live, you need to get a vacuum. Not only will it keep the carpet clean, but it will help to keep nasty germs from growing, help keep ants/cockroaches out, and will extend the life of your carpet as well.

2) **Plunger** – This is something that you want to have readily available when you need it. Otherwise, you're screwed.

3) **Toilet paper** – Keep a ready supply of this on hand. Nobody likes walking out of the bathroom missing a sock.

4) **Toilet Scrubber** – It's hard to impress your friends when there are poop streaks plastered all over the inside of your toilet. If you don't want your bathroom to look like you are trying to cultivate some type of mold for science, then you need to get a toilet scrubber.

5) **Paper towels** – These come in handy for just about

everything. You'll use them as napkins, to clean up spills, and for cleaning around the house as well. Make sure you have a supply of them readily available at all times.

6) **Lightbulbs** – These things will go out all the time, and if you have multiple of them that go bad in a day (it happens), you will be stuck in the dark. Keep a small supply of these available and you won't have to live in the dark.

7) **Swiffer** – One of mankind's greatest inventions. Swiffers absolutely rock. The dry cloths that you attach at the bottom do a great job of dusting up your floors, but the wet pads that you can attach at the bottom are fantastic. I use them to clean my kitchen and laminate floors throughout the house in lieu of mopping and they do a fantastic job with half of the hassle of a mop.

8) **Snow shovel** – This will depend on where you live, but if it ever snows where you live you need to make sure that you have one of these somewhere on your property. I actually prefer using a flat-head digging shovel instead. It does a superior job of getting up all of the slush and ice as well, and I can use it for more than one purpose.

9) **Putty scraper with spackle** – Eventually you're going to put a hole in the drywall. It just happens. A putty scraper with spackle helps to ensure that you can get the job done in a timely manner.

10) **Sandpaper** – I keep a variety of grits available at all times, but you could probably get by with 120 grit and 220 grit just fine. You'll be surprised at how often you end up using these in a home.

11) **Air filters** – Somewhere on your walls is going to be a gigantic rectangular vent. This is where your air filter goes, and you may have multiple vents like this throughout your house. If you open it up by sliding the little lock things at the top to the side, you'll be able to see what size air filter was in there before. It'll look dark and disgusting if it needs to be replaced. You can get replacement air filters at Walmart, Lowe's, or Home Depot. We change ours every 2 months or so. Not changing them out can be hard on your HVAC system, and will result in stuff floating around in your air that can aggravate your allergies.

12) **Carbon monoxide detector** – I recommend having at least two of these in your house. One for the kitchen, and one for your bedroom. Carbon monoxide is an odorless poisonous gas that will knock you unconscious and kill you if given the chance. Gas leaks into your home can cause these. A carbon monoxide detector lets out a terrifying screech when it detects the gas, letting you know that you need to vacate the premises and see what you can do to stop the leak.

How to Shop for Furniture

When shopping for furniture the first thing that I would recommend would be to get an idea of what the marketplace price is for the particular style of furniture that you are looking for. Furniture is a *big* purchase. It's something that can set you back several thousand dollars, and if you're just going to take the first sticker price that gets thrown your way, you're gonna get screwed.

You have to make sure that you know approximately what a particular piece of furniture should cost you. That being said though there are some specifics that you're going to want to consider when shopping for furniture.

Is it built solidly?

I worked at an office supply company for years growing up. My job was mainly to assemble and deliver furniture. As a result, I ended up getting a pretty good taste for what was top-notch furniture and what was cheap.

Ikea may be inexpensive, but I've found it to be rather poorly made. If you want something that's going to last, I recommend that you skip it. Look for something more genuine.

Is the furniture built out of real wood or particle board?

Real wood is stronger. Is it rickety? Does it creak a whole lot? Does it just look flimsy? If the answer to any of these questions is 'yes', then you're probably looking at cheap furniture. Buy quality and it can potentially last you a lifetime.

Is it sticker price?

If you shop at any of the furniture stores out there the price you see on the tag is going to be the sticker price. However, many times furniture is like cars. You can haggle for the price a bit.

Furniture salesmen often operate under commission. The more they sell, the more they make. They *want* to make the sale to you. As a result, they're often willing to weasel around with the price to make the sale. Be aware of this. Ask if there are any sales going on, or if there are discounts if you buy the ottoman *and* the chair.

If you don't like the prices that the salesman is giving you, then by all means leave. Odds are you can find something similar elsewhere, or that store will have a sale closer to your desired price soon.

Is it nasty?

Come on, why would you even consider buying a used mattress? That's about as gross as it gets. Fun fact: bedbugs can hide in furniture too. If you're buying used furniture with upholstery on it, just be aware of that. I'd personally rather buy the new couch than the old one, especially considering that statistics say somewhere around 99% of couples have had "alone" time on their couch.

If you're going to buy something with upholstery used, personally I would have it reupholstered and store it somewhere outside in the meantime. A used kitchen table would be a different story, as it's solid wood, but if it's an old upright fabric chair then that's what I would do.

There are options out there to find furniture at a much lower price.

There's always IKEA. I'm personally not a huge fan of it (I think it's cheap), but IKEA does make furniture that's easy to assemble and has a very low sticker price. It may help your residence to be more than just a mattress on the floor and a pile of clothes in the corner.

You can always make your own as well if you're more of the do-it-yourselfer. This can save you quite a bit of money if you're good with tools. Ana White has an excellent website with all kinds of DIY furniture plans that are shabby-chic style. I've used some of them and the furniture turned out great. Pinterest can be another great source of DIY cheap furniture plans.

How to Do Laundry

If you don't know how to do laundry by now, you are one of the millions of just-graduated men throughout the country. This isn't something that I would go around bragging about. It won't get you many dates.

I can't give people too much crap on this one though. I was the same way. It wasn't until I finally had graduated and gotten my first place to myself, with no roommates, that I finally realized it was high time to learn how to do my own laundry.

All through college, I would just save it to bring to my mom whenever I visited about once a month (sorry Mom). Gross? Yes. Irresponsible and callous of me? Yeah, probably that too. But I figured better late than never and learned what it was I needed to know.

Here is what I do to clean my laundry:

I always sort my clothes by color.

By that I mean all of the white clothes get separated by all of the clothes that are actually a color. Putting white clothes in with colored clothes can quickly result in clothes that are no longer white.

The color can leach off of the fabric of your new red shirt and turn all of your whitey-tighties into pink undies. Not the most masculine of colors.

Some people further sort their clothing into "lights" as well, meaning all of their lighter colors (pastels, yellow, orange, etc.) from the darker colors. I don't do this, but whatever floats your boat.

Lastly, you're going to want to sort out "delicates" as well, particularly if you're a woman. All your bras, lingerie, panties, and whatever else silky and all that you may have are going to need to be washed separately from the heavier clothes such as denim or you're going to beat the crap out of the delicate fabrics and potentially damage your clothes.

If you have any stained clothes, adding a stain remover will help you out A LOT.

Let's say you got grease on your khakis, wine on your dress shirt, or red clay on your jeans. In any of these cases, just a simple wash through the machine may not do the trick. It depends on what you use of course, but it doesn't hurt to pre-treat your stains.

We used OxiClean Max Stain Remover growing up, but now I just use Tide To Go Instant Stain Remover Pens for most stuff. Just spurt some of the stuff on the stain according to the directions on the bottle, and then throw it in the wash with the rest of your clothes.

Throw the pile of laundry in that you want to wash first, put the detergent in the detergent area, and press whatever buttons you need to press to get the washer to start.

Your washer is going to have different settings for different clothing options, but most of the time I just hit the 'Start' button and let the washer do its thing.

I'm a guy though, and most of what I wear is comprised of blue jeans, T-shirts, and hoodies. If you're a girl or somebody who has to wear dressier clothing on a regular basis for work, you may want to change up the settings for your clothes accordingly.

After the washer is done washing your clothes, place them in the dryer as soon as you can.

If you leave them in the washer overnight, you may end up having to wash everything again because it will smell mildewy. Drying right away will prevent this.

When you throw your clothes in the dryer, I always recommend throwing a dryer sheet in there as well.

Not only do they make your clothes smell fantastic, but they keep your clothes from being all static-y as well.

Don't dry your clothes at too high of a temperature.

Some clothing fabrics, particularly cotton can shrink pretty drastically if they are dried too hot.

Fold your clothes as soon as you can after the dryer is done.

If you wait too long, then the clothes will get wrinkly, and you'll have to iron everything. Khakis and dress shirts you'll probably have to iron anyway, but the rest of it will be ok if you can get it folded and put away quick enough, and this'll save you a lot of extra time and work.

How to Iron Clothes

Nobody likes being around a person who always gives the appearance of being a slob. If you don't iron your clothes, that is what you are going to look like. There is absolutely nothing professional or attractive about looking like you don't give a crap about the clothes that are on your back right now.

So how do you iron clothing?

To start with, you're going to have to leave the iron on for about 5 minutes to get it all heated up.

During that time, prep the clothes that you are about to iron by getting your first item up on the ironing board, or by separating the clothing by material. Different materials may need different temperatures on the iron to prevent them from becoming damaged. The iron will have a setting for different types of clothing most likely, so this isn't something that you have to stress about too much.

Start from the inside of the clothing and work your way towards the edges with the iron.

Think of it as pushing the wrinkles outside of the clothing. It takes little swipes to do this usually, in my experience, and make sure that you pick up the iron after every swipe or two so that the steam that has built up in it can dissipate. You'll hear it hiss and release a bunch of vapor when you pick it up from the clothing.

You'll often have to iron both sides of an article of clothing to make sure that it looks nice.

Just be aware of that.

Once you are done ironing that particular article of clothing, fold it or place it on a hanger right away.

Otherwise, you can just end up with a re-wrinkled shirt, and nobody likes to have to do work on something that they previously had just finished.

Once you're done, unplug the iron so you don't burn your house down and give it time to cool off completely before you put it back into storage.

I Want to Build Things with Tools but I Live in an Apartment!

I completely understand this one. It can be incredibly frustrating to not just want to build things but have a burning desire to build things (I'm passionate about furniture-making if you can tell) and to not be able to do so due to space and noise constraints.

There are ways that you can work around this, however. The first thing that you can always do is to ask around. You may have a friend or neighbor who has a woodshop that they would love to let you use provided you pay them a small fee, coffee, or just conversation.

Getting in touch with your local woodworker's club/guild can lead to openings as well. I'm a member of the woodworker's guild here in my community and am easily the youngest guy there. If you picture a bunch of retired dudes, and then a random young guy that's pretty much what it's like. It's funny to hear meeting after meeting how the members complain that there just aren't any young people getting involved in woodworking anymore. (They say this as they look your way. Just a heads up.) They talk about how they fear their craft is a dying art, and encourage members to find younger people to take under their wing and teach the craft to.

By searching Facebook (that's all the leaders of these

groups tend to know how to use. Seriously.) for these types of groups, you may find an opening that can lead to you not only have a space to work with tools, but also a mentor who will teach you the tricks of the trade along the way.

The next option, which is rarer, but is growing is to look for a builder's club. These are small workshops that are essentially nothing more than workspaces with tools for rent. Members pay a small monthly fee to be able to come in and use these tools for their projects at any time they please. This can be a great way to get access to tools and information without having to pay hundreds of dollars for top-notch tools.

Lastly, an extension cord and some sawhorses can open up a whole new world for you as well. Solely by attaching your extension cord to an outdoor outlet at your apartment, you can build a host of things utilizing the sawhorses with boards laid across as a workspace. I did this for about a year in our first townhouse, and while not ideal, it did allow me to build a fair amount. Plus it was cheap.

What to Do If You Move

If you thought moving was a pain because of all the heavy stuff that you had to lift, you were only half right. In my opinion, moving is a pain because of all the people you have to call to notify them that you're changing your address or discontinuing their service.

It's not fun to discover that you have a host of late fees applied to your account because your electricity bill (which was mailed to your old address) was never paid. So, here are a few things you should do if you are getting ready to move.

Cancel services with all of the utilities at your old address.

Electricity, water, propane, TV, internet, landlines – all of these companies need to know that you will no longer be at your old address anymore. Otherwise, they'll keep sending bills in your name.

Call other companies that send you bills to let them know you are moving.

Your insurance companies, credit card companies, banks, magazine subscriptions, and companies that you've worked for within the past 360 days all need to know that you are changing your address.

All the places that you've worked within the past year

need to know so that they can send your tax information to the right place when it comes time to file your taxes. You don't want that information not showing up and/or getting into the wrong person's hands.

Go to the USPS website and update your address with them.

This is actually federally required within a certain number of days within your move so make sure that you get this taken care of. This lets the government know where you are at so that they can send property tax bills and other similar fun bills your way.

This also will get all of the other random mail that you get to be forwarded to your correct address for a set period of time. So all of those coupons, magazines, and other things that you would normally get won't end up in the wrong mailbox.

Get your address changed on your driver's license.

You'll probably have to visit the Department of Motor Vehicles (DMV) for this one. It's not fun, but it's the law, and you need to do it.

Update your address on eBay, PayPal, Amazon, and any other online website that you use to purchase things regularly.

Otherwise, like me, you'll send all of the textbooks that you just bought online to a residence an hour and a half away.

Get all of the services at your new address put in your name.

If you want electricity, propane, TV, internet, or a landline at your new place you're going to have to call the respective companies and tell them to turn it on for you there.

Register to vote.

If you move you actually have to let the registrar's office know so that you can vote in the next election. I think it's stupid, but that's just the way it is. There's actually an election coming up in a few weeks that I can't vote for because I missed the registration deadline. You can do this online if you want, but if you're at the DMV anyway changing addresses and stuff, you can do it there too.

What to Do When the Power Goes Out

Where I live there are a lot of trees. Simultaneously, we get some pretty crazy wind here too. As a result, trees fall on power lines and the power goes out around here what seems 1-2x/year.

If the power just goes out for an evening, it's kind of an adventure. You're camping out in your own house. A break from the routine. You have to survive. But anything longer than an evening, and you quickly realize that your life has just changed pretty drastically, and you need to make some adjustments if you want things to continue to work.

Your first and foremost concern (unless it's bitterly cold), is your fridge. Without power, your fridge is no longer keeping the food inside of it cold. The cold air that's already in there will last a little while, but not forever. The more that you open the fridge doors too, the less time that food inside is going to stay cold. You don't want an entire fridge and freezer full of food to go bad. That costs money.

If you're a total cheapskate and attempt to eat that food that hasn't been refrigerated for several days all you're doing is setting yourself up for an illness, and whatever money you thought you had saved by eating the last of the mayonnaise will quickly be spent on doctor's offices, prescriptions, and missed wages. And that's if you're lucky. Food-borne illness can kill you. So it's nothing to fool around with.

Aside from the fridge food slowly beginning to spoil, your fridge is also going to slowly start to thaw. That means that whatever ice had accumulated in the freezer is now going to start to melt, and will gradually drip down onto your kitchen floor into a gigantic puddle. If you have cracks in the grout lines of your kitchen tile like I do, then that water seeps through the floor into the basement. Given enough time that water can cause some serious damage that you're going to end up paying for.

So, you want to make sure that your fridge is ok.

What are your options for the fridge though?

Fill it with bags of ice. – You can typically pick up a 10lb bag of ice at the grocery store for around $3. I buy as many bags as will fit in my fridge and freezer, and stuff them in. Your fridge is essentially a big insulated lunchbox. Just think of it as filling it full of really big ice packs like you do when you pack your lunch for work.

That ice isn't going to last forever though. Sure, it'll buy you an extra couple of hours, but that ice is going to eventually melt, and then you end up with the water leak problem all over again. Placing each ice bag into a trash bag can help to prevent some of this from happening though.

Do not open the fridge door – As I said, every time you open that door, the temperature of the fridge is going to increase drastically. It's hard to keep the fridge cold when you just let out all of the cold air that it had. If you need something, then go ahead and open it, but just understand the consequences of what it is you're doing.

Buy a generator – I made it 5 years without getting one of these. After the most recent power outage for 3 days though, I had had enough. I paid $300 at Sam's Club for a really decent generator that I keep outside (don't run a generator inside unless you want to die from carbon monoxide poisoning), that gives me extra peace of mind.

No more worrying about what I'll do if the power goes out. Now when it happens, I just hook the generator up to the fridge with an extension cord, turn the thing on, and then just make sure the generator has enough gas.

Eat the food – If you have expensive food in that fridge that you don't want to worry about going bad, you could always try to eat as much of it as you could before it goes bad. You may end up eating deli meat for all three meals one day, but it's an option.

Let the food go bad and report it to your homeowner's insurance – A lot of homeowner's or renter's insurance policies will actually cover the food that you lose due to a power outage. I'd be hesitant to jump on this though because it may raise your insurance rates. If you lose $80 worth of food, but your insurance jumps $100 a year, is it really worth it?

If it's super cold outside, then keeping you and your place warm is probably going to be your most important priority. A house that gets too cold can end up with frozen pipes. And pipes that freeze tend to explode and make a big mess, spewing water throughout your whole house for what always seems to be hours and hours before you get home from work.

What can you do to keep your house warm?

- 1) If you have a propane fireplace (gas logs), it may be worth running them to get a marginal level of heat in your house – Gas logs don't require electricity to run. All you have to do is turn on the gas and then ignite it.
- 2) Gas space heaters – You'll see these for sale around town in the wintertime. Just make sure you know what you're doing if you use these. Don't burn your house down. I personally avoid these, but hey, it is an option.
- 3) Put pipe wraps around any exposed piping you can find.
- 4) Leave the faucets dripping.

Other things that really help

When the power goes out, life really gets pared down fast. You realize how important the little things like heat and A/C are. However, there are a lot of other things out there that will make life much, much more enjoyable at your place should the power go out.

- **Candles** – It's not always fun or practical to go to

bed when the sun dictates. Candles are one of the best ways to ensure that you do have some type of light in your place when the power goes down. Just make sure that you have some unscented ones that you keep in a closet somewhere. Having 12 different scents competing for air is a guaranteed way to make you nauseous.

- **Matches/Lighters** – You gotta have a way to light those candles, don't ya?
- **Blankets** – If your power goes out in the winter and you opt to stay at home, then you need to have plenty of spare blankets at hand. It's hard to sleep when you're freezing. I've tried.
- **LED lanterns** – I pick these things up at Walmart every now and then. They work fantastic. They run for hours and hours, don't use a lot of batteries, and really give off a lot of light. You can typically find them for around $20. I keep 'em in the bathroom when the power goes out because it's no fun guessing when you've actually finished wiping your butt.
- **Flashlights** – If you need to move around from room to room, carrying a candle doesn't exactly cut it. Make sure you have a couple of flashlights available.
- **Food that doesn't require cooking** – If you don't have power, odds are you can't cook. By keeping plenty of ready-to-eat foods such as bread, peanut butter, fruit, crackers, nuts, and the like on hand at all times, you help to ensure that you can actually eat a meal that doesn't contain cold soup when you're hungry. I always have a backpacking stove ready as well, which opens a lot more options. The key with it though is to never use it indoors unless

you want to die from carbon monoxide poisoning.
- **Purell** – No power most likely means that your water isn't going to work. It's always a good idea to clean your hands somehow before you eat, and in the case of a power outage, Purell will cover this gap for you. I keep it by all the sinks during outages.

Random Tips on Power Outages

As we already mentioned, when the power goes out, odds are that your water is going to quit working as well. If you're on a well, the pump that brings water up out of the well to you runs on electricity. If you live in the city, you're most likely on city water, and wherever the water is coming from may be an area that wasn't affected by the outage.

Toilets

What does this mean for you though? Well, with no water, it can be hard to flush the toilets. This quickly becomes a nightmare in the middle of July heat and you've got a toilet full of stinky crap. You can still flush the toilet though. The water exiting from your house leaves via gravity. Gravity never stops, and as a result you can still flush your toilet in a power outage. Where you're going to have trouble is with getting the toilet refilled with water.

You've probably already got 1-3 flushes worth of water stored in the tank right above your toilet. Fun fact: that water's technically drinkable as well. If your toilet runs out of water, just take the lid off of the top tank, and refill it with whatever water you have available. Voila. Your toilet can now effectively flush stuff again.

Bathing

When you haven't had power in 8 days, you have to get creative with how you stay clean. Here are the best options that I've found.

- First and foremost, you can always call a friend who still has power. If you're not too far away from them, and they have a shower that works, that's gonna be your best bet.
- If you just moved to a new town and don't know anybody, or if none of your friends have power either, your local gym is going to be the next best bet, provided you have a membership there. Pretty much every gym out there is going to have some type of shower facility available. And if you're already paying for the membership, you might as well use it.
- Large truck stop gas stations such as Flying J, Love's, and the like will have shower facilities available as well. They normally charge a few bucks, and you're going to have to wait for your ticket number to be called, but they are an option. Just make sure you bring some type of sandal to wear in that shower
- Campgrounds will have showers a lot of times as well. Again though, there's often a charge of a few bucks. However, if all of the above options are out, you're probably stuck with some type of rag bath using baby wipes or something like that. Most certainly not ideal, but if all of the above options don't

work, really what other option do you have?

LIFE

Ahhh...the school of life.

It's like being slapped upside the head with a wet fish. For all those other, random aspects of life that don't really have a good place to fit, we have them here. This is the confusing, garbled facets of life that are going to make you wish that you could live as a recluse in a cabin in the woods.

Part of that problem though is due to nobody having ever *taught* you these subjects before. Figuring them out on your own is about as frustrating as it gets. But you can't give up – this is stuff you need to know. And hopefully, I can help.

All About Insurance

Insurance in America is something that has been changing quite a bit as of late so I'm just going to hit you with the basics. Odds are that everything is going to change radically again here soon, but as long as you know a few basic guidelines and pieces of terminology you'll have a much better understanding of what you're paying for.

To start with, what exactly is insurance?

Insurance is basically a guarantee that should something terrible happen to you somebody else will pay for it (or at least a sizeable portion of it) because you have been paying a "membership fee" if you will to that insurance company all along.

There are multiple different types of insurance that you can purchase, and I do think that there are some types that you should have.

Let's start with the big one, health insurance.

With health insurance, you will pay the insurance company a certain amount every month so that should you get sick, break a bone, need an MRI, or whatever, the insurance company will pay for some (maybe all) of the medical bill.

Up until this point, your parents most likely covered any medical expenses that you may have received. Now though you're an adult and you're on your own. If you do end up going to a hospital anytime soon you will be absolutely blown away with how much the sticker price is later.

Medical bills are expensive and without health insurance, you can end up deep deep deep in debt very fast.

All about copays

Insurance has its own language, and copays are going to be one of the most common terms you'll see thrown around in the insurance world. A copay is a small fee that you will pay every time you use your insurance. $25 is a pretty standard amount, but depending on the plan you have it could be more or less.

What that $25 copay means is that every time you go to the doctor's office, you will end up paying the $25 copay. The insurance from that point will foot the rest, or at least most of the rest of the bill.

What are dependents?

Dependents is another term thrown around in the insurance world. A dependent is somebody who depends on you. This is typically a spouse or kids. In the insurance world, a dependent is somebody who you would like to have covered under your medical insurance on top of yourself. So if you're married with 1 kid, you'll want to purchase insurance for yourself with 2 dependents.

If your spouse works full time and you have a kid, your spouse may be able to get a cheaper insurance rate through their own company than being joined under your policy. In that case, your spouse has their policy, and you'll have yours with one dependent – your kid. That may end up getting you a much cheaper rate than having everybody under your insurance plan.

The more dependents you have under your plan, the higher the insurance plan is gonna cost you, so just be aware of that as well.

What's a beneficiary?

A beneficiary is the person who benefits from your death. We're not talking about your mortal enemy here, but instead about life insurance. If you have a life insurance policy, you'll have beneficiaries listed under it. This means that if you've purchased a $10,000 life insurance policy and listed your spouse as the beneficiary, your spouse will 'benefit' by receiving the $10,000 policy after you die.

Dental insurance

Given the option from your employer's benefits package, I would recommend buying this one. It often is incredibly cheap (less than $10/month) and if you go to the dentist twice a year (as I believe you should) then the insurance will cover the costs. This type of insurance may even make your twice-annual cleanings "free". And in the event that you have a cavity, need a root canal, or lose a tooth playing hockey then the insurance will pay the majority of the $600 bill.

Vision insurance

If you have glasses or contacts, vision insurance is another form of insurance that I highly recommend that you can often get for around $10/month. It will help to cover the cost of your eye doctor appointments and may get you a free pair of glasses every year as well. If you currently don't have a need for prescriptive lenses, then you can probably get by without paying for this one.

Car insurance

Different states have different laws regarding car insurance, but it basically works like this. Should you be in an accident that is not your fault, you'll be covered. Somebody else will pay all of the bills you receive.

Should you be involved in an accident that is your fault (it happens) the insurance company will cover part of the cost for your repairs as well as the victim's repairs. And should that victim end up needing medical attention you'll be incredibly thankful that you have car insurance because you're going to pay for all of those bills too.

If you end up rear-ending somebody at a light and that person ends up with chronic back pain that requires MRIs, chiropractor appointments, pain medicine, and physical therapy you will be incredibly grateful to have car insurance that will pay for that guy's medical costs. Because without it, you'll pay for it and it could drive you into a financial hole you will have an incredibly difficult time digging yourself out of.

Renter's insurance

Odds are that your first place is going to be something

that you rent. When this is the case there can be times when accidents happen to the rental property that damage your stuff. For example, if the gigantic oak tree right over the house you're renting falls onto your house late at night and smashes your laptop.

When things like this happen, then the insurance company will cover any of the costs for damages.

Property insurance

Property insurance is essentially what renter's insurance is. It insures your stuff against damages. If you ever do have to make a claim stating that some of your stuff was damaged, there is one thing that you can do to make your life a whole lot easier: take pictures or a video of your stuff beforehand.

We had a pretty bad tornado here where I live not too long ago. Many of the affected families weren't fully reimbursed by their insurance companies for loss of property. Why? Because the insurance company wanted picture proof that the families actually owned the items that they were claiming.

It was absolutely ridiculous. First, who takes pictures of their stuff, and second, if a tornado damaged your house, wouldn't there be a pretty good chance that those pictures would be gone too? Similarly, what's the point of paying for property insurance if you're not allowed to use it?

As a result, I recommend taking a video/pictures and updating it to the cloud so just in case something ever does happen, you have visible proof that you did indeed own the item that was damaged. It'll save you a lot of headaches and heartache down the road should something terrible ever happen to your stuff such as theft, fire, flood, or who knows what else.

Life insurance

This is one that I think is a good idea even if you don't have a wife, kids, or provide for somebody.

Life insurance gives a big chunk of change to whoever you designate it to should you die. It can be a great way to make sure that your spouse is taken care of financially should something happen to you. Funeral costs in and of themselves are prohibitively expensive, so you're going to want something to take care of that.

However, if you like the idea of that significant person in your life to be able to pay off a lot of debt, have funds to live off of for a little while, not have to worry about finances while they're mourning, or be able to have a chunk of cash to pay for college/a business/whatever then life insurance is also a good idea.

If you're just starting out, you'll probably be able to get this for pretty cheap.

There are two main types of life insurance that you can look at: term life insurance and permanent life insurance.

Term life insurance is something that you can often purchase through your employer's benefits package for a small fee each month. With term life insurance, a set fee will come out of each paycheck automatically. You can purchase different amounts of life insurance with it, with larger insurance amounts costing a larger fee. So a $20,000 life insurance policy that gives whoever you designate as the beneficiary on the paperwork $20,000 when you die may cost something like $14/month. A $10,000 policy may only cost $5/month. The higher the amount, the higher the rate.

The only negative about term life insurance is that the rate can change from year to year. So you may only end up paying $14/month for this year, but next year that may go up to $16/month for the exact same policy.

Permanent life insurance is a little different. With permanent life insurance, you want to buy it when you're young and keep it for the rest of your life. The rate with this stuff never changes. Younger people tend to be healthier than older people. Older people tend to die, younger people tend to live. Insurance companies recognize this, and as a result, older people will pay a higher rate for life insurance than younger people will.

A 70-year-old man could end up dying tomorrow. As a result, if he wants to own a $20,000 life insurance policy, he's going to end up paying a premium for it. Just as an example, we'll say he pays $300/month for it.

A 22-year-old is likely to live for a very long time. If he wants to own a $20,000 life insurance policy, the insurance company is willing to give him a much lower rate because they aren't as afraid that he's going to die tomorrow and they're going to have to shell out $20,000.

As a result, the 22-year-old may only end up paying $14/month for that policy.

Here's why this type rocks though.

If that 22-year-old signs on for that $20,000 policy of permanent life insurance, and he stays signed up to it for his whole life, he can end up being 95 years old but still locked into the same rate of $14/month.

That's freakin' fantastic.

Other 95-year-olds would pay hundreds of dollars a month for that same policy.

I highly recommend getting this type of policy and hanging on to it. Get term life insurance too if you want, but definitely make sure you can get a permanent rate life insurance policy if you can swing it. It's a minimum amount that you'll pay, and it'll make sure that the people you love are taken care of when you die.

Morbid? Maybe, but it is a very wise, thoughtful, and good thing to do to not leave your spouse/kids/parents left behind with all of your medical and funeral costs, and the money can help them to make sure that they are taken care of for a while.

How to Small Talk Without Being Awkward

I consider myself pretty proficient now with small talk. But holy smokes, did I used to hate to do it before I figured out the secrets to it. I can remember when I was around 15 working in my dad's office product company absolutely dreading having "grownups" walk by. 100% of the time they would walk by and for some reason feel the need to say *something*, and it ended up being just awkward empty clichés EVERY time.

"Can't you say something with meaning?!"

Ugg. I hated it, and I still hate it. Small talk without meaning anyway.

I do believe that there is a way to show that you are much more than an inspirational poster when you come into contact with people on a daily basis. A way to be *authentic* without being overwhelming in everyday small conversation.

What I've found to be one of the keys is to be observant.

When I first started personal training, my initial job interview consisted of walking the floor and proving I could talk to complete strangers. Being observant was what got me that job.

For example, when I saw somebody wearing a T-shirt with a restaurant or city name on it, I would ask them if they had been there. That would typically start up a conversation. The person would want to tell me about how great the food was there, how they always vacation in that town with their family, or whatever.

It turns out this is actually a sneaky salesman tactic that I had stumbled across. I've had a number of different pyramid scheme suckers start up conversations with me using the exact same method. They got me talking about the place on my T-shirt and I completely let my guard down. It wasn't until they started trying to recruit me that I realized what was going on, and understood the genius of the T-shirt idea.

I don't normally open up about life in the grocery store to complete strangers, but holy smokes those people got me to completely let my guard down without having any clue. I just thought they were being nice. Now I'm not saying that you want to be the creepy recruiter guy, but the ability to observe what that particular person is interested in and make conversation about it is something that will enable you to talk with people about anything.

The second key is to remember past conversations.

If the person isn't a complete stranger, you can often mine info from past conversations to know what they like to talk about. People want to know that other people not only care about them but think that they are interesting as well. When you ask somebody how the auction was that they went to this past weekend, if their dog has dug through the drywall again recently, or how their corn is growing they will immediately open up.

Why? Because you have shown an interest in their own lives. And when you do that, people will open up.

The third key is to pay attention to current events.

This is something I learned as a personal trainer, and it helped me a ton. I would flip on the news real quick every morning for 5 minutes just to catch a glimpse of what was happening in the world. Talking politics may not be the best idea at work, but the news is so much more than just politics. There are always natural disasters, criminals in your neighborhood, or just strange happenings that can be used as the key to unlocking a light-hearted non-heated conversation with somebody.

I always start these conversations by saying something along the lines of, "Did you hear about…I saw it on the news this morning." Easy conversation starter right there. I like the strange news the best. For example, there was recently a bank worker that got locked inside an ATM machine and was handing out "Help Me, I'm trapped inside" notes to people as they drove through. It took several cars until somebody finally realized it wasn't a joke. I had a blast with people talking about what must have been going through that guy's head.

Finding funny or weird little stories like that can help you talk to anyone.

The fourth key is to tell a story about something stupid that happened to you.

This one will probably get me made fun of a little, but I still think that it's a great way to initiate conversation, especially before the awkward silence grips the room. For some reason I have a plethora of stupid things that I do or that happen to me on a daily basis. I am regularly getting locked out of my house, having to chase a chicken through a neighbor's yard, or getting kicked in the shin by random toddlers as they pass me down the aisle at Walmart.

Starting a conversation by saying, "You know what happened to me the other day?", and then going from there into the meat of the silly story will help the person to laugh or smile. They'll see the same humor in the situation that you saw. Humor is one of the quickest ways to get somebody to feel at ease. When people feel at ease, they talk.

Using a bit of humor can often help you to start that conversation that you've been looking for.

The final key is to always have an individualized answer when somebody asks "How are you?/How's it going?"

Any idiot can reply with "good" and let the conversation die with that. It takes somebody who knows how to work with people to actually give an update. You don't want to give a life story, and you don't want to give a sob story. The person was initiating small talk. They don't want your sob story.

Tell them what you actually have been up to lately. "Well, I've been working on building a farmhouse table for my wife. Getting the top to squish together right is a lot harder than I thought it would be." An answer like that is going to allow the conversation to flourish. It leads to further questions, which lead to further conversation.

The Rules of Social Media

You would think that people would know these by now, but they don't. Social media can be a wonderful thing. But it can also get you into a world of headache, heartache, and trouble if you're not careful. Here are the basic rules that you need to know before posting anything to social media:

It's not a journal.

If you want to keep a journal of how you are feeling about the things that are going on in your life, that's fine. Do it in a journal. Don't publish everything that you feel online for the world to see. Why? For starters, it makes you look tacky. You'll come across as overly sensitive and whiny to all of your online friends.

It can also get you in trouble. Let's say that you think your boss is a jerk and post it online for the world to know. There's a very good possibility that your boss will find out about that post. Keep your feelings somewhere where only you can see them and they won't get you into trouble with your boss.

If you talk politics, expect potentially sharp replies.

There's nothing wrong with talking politics. It's one of the great things about freedom of speech: you can share your ideas with anybody without fear of repercussion. I have no problem with people talking politics on social media either. Just understand that if you do so there's an almost 100% guarantee that there will be somebody who will disagree with you. And they will let you know. Loudly.

Don't let these conversations drag you into a heated argument. It's ok to debate a bit, just don't get permanently upset that somebody replied to your post differently than you think they should.

Avoid online arguments.

Oh boy, is there anything more embarrassing than an online argument? It's hard to tell. They just make all of the participants look stupid. If you're going to argue, do it in person. Don't share embarrassing secrets and attempt to destroy somebody's character and reputation in front of the entire online world.

Don't post your current location.

If you want to show the world some of the pics from your latest mountaineering expedition that's fine. Just do it after you're already home. A lot of people don't understand this, or just don't think that it's that important of a concept, but when you are posting your current location for the entire world to see, somebody may show up at your current location who you would much prefer not to. It could be the crazy ex-boyfriend. It could be the guy looking for a fight. It could be the guy looking to rape you.

Seriously. It may sound far-fetched, but that stuff has happened before to people who thought the same thing. Nobody ever expects to be kidnapped, raped, or murdered, yet it happens every day. It's best to not let the crazy and wicked people of the world know where you're gonna be at any particular time.

Sharing your location also tells the entire world where you are not. Particularly, it could tell everybody that you're not at your house. If you are not at your house and all your expensive stuff is, then it makes it that much easier for the bad guy to rob you while you're away. Coming back from vacation to an absolutely destroyed and pillaged home is not a fun process. Avoiding posting your current locations can help to keep that from happening.

Don't post embarrassing pictures of yourself or your friends.

Nobody enjoys the world being able to see a picture that makes them look like an idiot. You don't either. So don't do that to your friends.

Aside from just the embarrassing ones, don't post one that could potentially embarrass yourself in the future. Nobody needs to see your boob, dick hair, or the curves of your butt that you're showing off for in the mirror. You are not a prostitute, you do not want to be one, and you don't want to attract the kind of people around you who would like a prostitute.

Keep your pictures of yourself and your friends classy. Not only will your employer see these pictures (we often Facebook snoop before hiring somebody), but your future spouse may look at them as well, and they (along with their entire family and friend base) will judge your character based on what they find.

Don't post pictures of yourself with a drink in your hand.

This is just something that makes you look like an alcoholic, immature, and that you don't know how to handle responsibility. Keep your profile classy. Once again, your boss and future spouse will look at these pictures.

Don't post pictures of yourself doing drugs.

You would think this one would be obvious, but I've seen too many of my online friends doing it to persuade me otherwise. This is a good way to end up in jail.

Don't post your address, email, or phone number.

If you don't think it's fun receiving creepy letters or messages from blocked numbers and strangers, I would highly recommend that you skip this one. If you need to share your contact info with somebody by all means do it via private message.

Aside from the creeper aspect of this one, doing this makes you an easy target for the idiot friend or pissed-off ex who thinks it would be funny to subscribe you to every hard porn website/newsletter that they can.

Don't threaten *anyone* in your posts.

This is a surefire way to wind up in jail. Threatening the president or a politician will land you in jail, and threatening somebody you're in an argument with will too. If you have issues with somebody, take it up with them in person and try to avoid doing anything during that conversation that will land you in jail as well.

Basic Etiquette

Sorry, but to put it bluntly many of your parents have failed you on this one. Maybe you just refused to listen. Either way, you do not want to come across as a pompous, insensitive, egomaniac. Here are some of the basic rules of etiquette that you should practice daily.

1) **Hold the door for people behind you** – This is most definitely a Southern thing, but it is also the correct thing. Letting the door slam in the face of somebody behind you is rude.

2) **Say 'Please' and 'thank you'** – You did this as a little kid, do it as an adult too.

3) **Understand conversation etiquette** – Do not interrupt people, do not tell long-winded pointless stories, and give just the right amount of information when asked a question. People want to know the answer to their question, not your entire life's backstory.

4) **Don't one-up peoples' stories** – This is not endearing.

5) **Be on time** – This shows that you respect other people's time.

6) **Do what you say you will** – If you do not honor your word, you cannot be trusted, and I do not want you around.

7) **Do not ask rude questions** – If it's not your business, it's not your business. Curiosity killed the cat, and it can kill a friendship before it ever gets the chance to develop too.

8) **Introduce people** – If you are in a conversation with somebody and your friend who doesn't know that somebody is present, introduce them to each other. It's awkward for both of them otherwise.

9) **Don't have public phone conversations** – Nobody wants to hear your annoying phone conversation. Especially if they are a captive audience. It makes for the longest elevator ride ever which is aggravating on so many levels (thank you, I'll be here all week).

10) **Tell people they're on speakerphone** – Otherwise, they may say something they will regret, and you will have publicly humiliated them.

Basic Dinner Etiquette

Let's say your boss, your girlfriend's family, your first date, or just a friend invites you over to their place for dinner and it is going to be a formal occasion. You cannot treat the place like it is your own, and you cannot have the meal completely oblivious to any of the rules of etiquette if you don't want to come across as ungrateful, rude, or a slob.

Now I by no means claim to be an etiquette professional. But I do claim to have been born, and raised in the South where etiquette matters. Here are the main rules of dinner etiquette that you should follow:

Dress decent – You don't have to necessarily show up in a suit and tie (unless it is that kind of event), but you should not just show up in paint-covered jeans and an old stained T-shirt with holes. Dress in a way that you will be comfortable but that shows that you do give a care and respect the company of those around you.

Don't criticize the food, location, or host – You will only offend those around you and come across as ungrateful.

Wait until all are served to start eating – Otherwise, you come across as self-absorbed.

Don't burp – Gross.

Pace yourself. Don't finish well before everybody else –

Wolfing down your food and finishing before everybody else makes it look like the host did not prepare enough food for you. This only puts both of you in an uncomfortable and awkward situation that they will not appreciate.

Don't get drunk. – Sounds like common sense, but trust me, it happens.

Bring a hostess gift – This is a time-trusted technique that will get you places. Bringing a small, thoughtful gift to the hostess shows that you not only have class, but that you do truly appreciate the work that the host/hostess has put into preparing this meal for you. A bottle of wine, scented candle, or small item that is reminiscent of your hometown will show that you have put some serious thought into preparing for this meal.

Say thank you for the meal – Show your gratitude.

Do not smack your food in your mouth – If you do this at my house I will be slamming your head into the table over and over again in my imagination while smiling and making polite conversation in reality.

Do not talk with food in your mouth – Rude and gross.

Don't voice your dietary beliefs/inhibitions now – Sure, maybe you think eating meat is evil. But voicing that opinion after the host has prepared you a wonderful meatloaf dinner only makes everybody embarrassed. The French have a saying that the man with dietary restrictions makes a terrible guest. Don't be the terrible guest.

Avoid your phone – You are there to spend time with them. Using your phone makes it look like you do not value their company.

Learn how to hold a frickin' fork and spoon – Holy smokes, is eating a meal with somebody who holds their silverware like an ignorant caveman annoying or what? *Did your mother never teach you how to eat?!*

Do not ask for seasoning that is not available – And don't season your food before you have tasted it as well. Both of these actions assume that what the host has made for you does not taste good as is, and must be doctored by a number of different seasonings or sauces.

Eat cleanly – This is not the time to end up with food all over your mouth and clothes. If given the choice, don't order foods that are notoriously messy such as hot wings.

Don't eat the last of something – This not only makes it look as if the host did not prepare enough food for you but also makes it look as if you only think about your own stomach.

Don't sit at the head of the table – The head of the table is the seat of honor. DO NOT SIT IN IT. This is where the host or head of the house sits. Choose a seat that is somewhere in the middle of the table, or wherever the host directs you to sit.

Don't ask for seconds if it is not appropriate – Use discretion to know the level of appropriateness. Asking for seconds when none are offered makes it look as if the host did not cook enough for you to be satisfied.

Don't be a jerk to the waiter – Give them extra slack at these meals. You do not want to be perceived as an insensitive, impatient, and hateful jerk. Watching somebody at my table be hateful towards the waiter makes me very angry very quickly and is embarrassing to the rest of the group.

Tips on Buying an Engagement Ring

You've finally met the perfect girl, and after getting to know each other for quite a bit of time, you're confident that she is the one. Now it's time to pick out the ring, but where do you even begin? You don't want to buy something that looks like it just came out of a gumball machine, but the bags of ramen noodles all over your kitchen are proof that you can't buy a rock. Plus, the fake stuff looks so real now. How do you know that you're getting a quality diamond for a reasonable price?

After weeks of research, I finally found the perfect engagement ring for my wife...at a pawn shop. Yeah, that sounds like the cheap way to go, but I actually got a beautiful setting with quality diamonds for a very reasonable price. And my fiancée (now wife) loves it.

So where do you start?

Your typical engagement ring is going to be a clear, colorless diamond, and that's actually the color of gem chosen in close to 90% of wedding rings.

Your current girlfriend/future fiancée may want something different color wise such as her birthstone or something like that, but unless she's explicitly stated she hates clear diamonds, they're probably going to be your best bet.

When it comes to engagement ring shopping, you need to know the 4 "C"s of diamonds: color, cut, clarity, and carat.

Color

Color refers to the color of the diamond (duh). Diamonds can have different tints to them. Just like all human teeth are white, some people have white teeth, some people have yellow teeth, and the rest fall somewhere in between. The clearer the diamond is, the less tint it has to it, typically the higher the cost. There's a bit of a personal preference in this one as well. Your future wife may not want a urine yellow diamond, but will barely be able to tell the difference between some of the higher grade color ratings.

Cut

Cut refers to the shape of the diamond. There are approximately 10 basic shapes that diamonds are typically cut into with round being the most popular choice. As a result, though, it often tends to be more expensive as well.

According to the numbers you can often save something like 40% by choosing any other shape other than round.

If you're anything like I was when I was shopping for a wedding ring, you're currently flat broke. My entire life savings went into that ring, and when I showed the jeweler what I wanted and what I had he literally looked at me and laughed. I don't shop there anymore. So, if you're strapped for cash going with a princess cut (a square) or a pillow cut (rounded square) could help make getting that ring much more of a reality.

Clarity

Clarity refers to how perfect the diamond is. Are there imperfections in there or not? The more imperfections that are in the diamond, the cheaper the diamond will be. You can cut some corners on this one. Absolutely nobody that I have met has asked my wife or me what the clarity grading of her diamond is. It's almost impossible to tell perfect diamonds with the naked eye. Yeah, you probably aren't going to want the lowest grade diamond. You want there to be some brilliance to it, but don't fret too much about diamond clarity.

Carat

Carat refers to the size of the diamond. The larger the carat, the larger the diamond, and consequentially the larger the price tag. You want to find something that looks respectable on her finger (no girl wants to show off a microscopic stone to her friends), but that won't break the bank as well. Shop around to find what carat size you can reasonably expect to be able to afford.

Ok, cool. So now we know a bit about diamonds and what we should look for on a quality scale to make sure that we don't get ripped off, but how do we know that she'll like it without asking her, and where do we buy them to get a good deal?

Nobody wants to ruin the surprise of an engagement. I certainly didn't. So I turned to one of mankind's greatest inventions: Pinterest. To my utter glee, my wife had a board pinned 'Wedding'. She'd been posting to it since high school with different ideas she liked. On that board, there were a number of different rings that she had pinned that helped me to know what style she liked.

If she doesn't have Pinterest or hasn't pinned this stuff in the past, you're going to either have to ask her close friends/family or just wing it. Her friends and family may have some good ideas, but if you just wing it please, please, please don't get something 'unique just like her'. If you're going to wing it, stick with a more classic design like a round solitaire quality diamond in a white gold band.

As far as where to go to shop for the ring goes, I ended up getting mine from a very nice pawn shop in the area. The words "pawn shop" may fill your mouth with a bitter flavor, but don't toss the idea away yet. After shopping through a number of jewelers you may quickly realize that pawn shops are suddenly becoming a much more attractive idea.

Your traditional jeweler can be great. They can get you virtually any type of ring you want, and if they don't have the type you want in-store they can actually customize a ring for you. But in my experience jewelers are often very expensive. The sales staff is commission based often too, and this can result in some less than stellar experiences. For example, I had a ring ordered from a particular jeweler that I ended up canceling my order on. Why? Because the price that we agreed on continued to climb as time went on. If you can't honor your original agreement, you've lost my business.

I searched every jeweler within my area of the state it seemed. The best-priced ones in my opinion were Henebrey's and Fink's. If you have those in your area, I think they're worth a shot.

Going back to pawn shops though, you'd be surprised at what you can find there. There are a lot of different rings there, and even if it's not in the correct size for your wife, a jeweler can easily resize the ring for a reasonable fee of under $100. The pricing is going to be much more affordable as well compared to a jeweler, and the ring will be just as good as new.

Random Relationship Tips

Look, I'm certainly no relationship guru. I don't have all the answers. But what I do have is the benefit of having been in a relationship for quite a bit of time now, and I've had even longer to observe the relationships of others. I've watched enough relationships go down the tube for incredibly stupid reasons to understand that there are some basic principles of having a special relationship with somebody else that people tend to be oblivious to. Below is some of what I've learned.

You'll notice that most all of them come directly from the Bible. That's because I'm a Christian, and I've found that the Bible is hands down the best source of relationship advice out there.

The grass isn't greener on the other side.

I asked an older man once what he knew now that he wished he knew back when he was my age. He thought for a second and then said, "I've got a 45-year-old daughter that will no longer speak to me. The grass isn't always greener on the other side. I wish I had known that then."

Here was a guy that had ruined his life by cheating on his wife. When times get hard in your relationship (and I'm sorry, but they will), you've got to remember that the grass isn't greener on the other side because there is going to be the temptation to believe it is. It's when you start to believe that your character, reputation, and relationship are tragically damaged.

Love languages differ.

If you haven't already, you need to read *The 5 Love Languages* by Gary Chapman. This book details how there are actually 5 different languages in which people express and feel loved. They are physical touch, quality time, words of encouragement, acts of service, and giving gifts.

If you or your partner isn't feeling very loved at the moment, you need to take a closer look at both of your personalities. Your partner may be doing all kinds of acts of service for you, and therefore thinking that your love tank is full, but if they haven't given you the words of encouragement that you so desperately need then you're going to feel unloved and underappreciated.

Understanding these differences can really help you to avoid a lot of needless arguments and hurtful words down the road.

Remember at all times what you truly want, and let your decisions move from there.

This truth comes from the book *Communicating for a Change*. Why on earth they never had us read this book in any of my comms classes in high school or college I'll never know, because it is hands down the best book out there on the subject.

I tend to be incredibly skeptical when faced with these

types of books. *I don't need to read this. Just act like a decent human being and everything will be fine.* Yeah, but the problem is that being a decent human being is incredibly hard at some times. When faced with conflict and escalating discussions, this book tells you what you need to know to actually have a true love-centered discussion.

The key? Remember what the end goal is and move from there.

The end goal is I want my wife and me to be close to each other. A lot of times the way we handle conflict does not have that end goal anywhere in the picture. I don't truly want to solely be right and to have my wife think I'm an obnoxious prick. I want us to have a rock-solid relationship filled with easily visible love. That doesn't mean that you behave like a door mat and let people walk all over you. It doesn't mean that you are always wrong or always need to be the one to apologize.

It does mean that you have to remember what you truly want to get that relationship though.

Don't go to bed angry .

This one comes straight from Ephesians 4:26. "Do not let the sun go down on your wrath, nor give place to the devil." Going to bed angry only allows time for both of you to fume and imagine all the ways that you hate the other person. Nothing ends up being resolved, problems only fester. You can't let yourself go to bed angry. That doesn't mean that you have to resolve the problem overnight. Many times that's impossible. You don't just make a gigantic decision that affects the both of you such as adoption, moving, job changes, or the like over the course of one night, nor should you.

What you do need to do though is make sure that at the end of each night you let the other person know that you do truly love them, you value their input, and that you are going to get through this decision together and emerge even stronger on the other side.

Doing that is what keeps the devil from getting a foothold in your relationship where he can further drive a wedge and destroy what you have completely.

Speak the truth in love (Eph 4:15)

Holy smokes, am I blown away by how many times people remain oblivious to this. *"But I told her the truth! Isn't that what I'm supposed to do? She shouldn't be upset!"* It's often not what you say, but how you say it. If you want your significant other to know that you do truly care about them but need to communicate a message that may offend them, you need to speak the truth in love.

You're smart enough to figure this one out on your own. It's when you fail to do this that your relationship will suffer.

Love forgives.

This is by far the hardest one on this list. Because sometimes the person who has your heart in their hand is going to do or say something that cuts you to the core. You are going to be *deeply* hurt, and wonder where to go from there.

Now I'm not talking about physical abuse or anything like that. If that is happening you need to get out. What I am talking about is the stuff that will happen to you because you are in a relationship with an imperfect human being.

If you really want to delve into the nuts and bolts of this I highly recommend Brian Zahnd's *Unconditional*.

People make mistakes. People are stupid. But true love is able to forgive.

Proverbs 10:12 – "love covers all sins."

Proverbs 17:9 – "He who covers a transgression seeks love, but he who repeats a matter separates friends."

Freakin' shut up .

Far too many relationships end up in trouble because somebody doesn't know when to shut their mouth. It's when you can't do this that you end up really hurting somebody, and they may not be willing to forgive you as quickly as you would like.

I'm not saying that you need to be a closed book about everything. If anything, that can make things bad too. Your partner will feel distant from you. What I am saying is that you need to think some things through before you just let loose automatic gunfire.

Proverbs 10:19 – "In the multitude of words sin is not lacking, but he who restrains his lips is wise."

Proverbs 29:11 – "A fool vents all his feelings, but a wise man holds them back."

Nip it in the bud.

I've noticed that a lot of problems arise from imaginary perceptions that are allowed to fester into something twisted given enough time. This is when you need to speak the truth into your partner's life. When they let you know how they feel about something and that it is making them feel a certain not-good way towards you, you need to nip it in the bud.

This is especially the case when you know that what they are believing is a twisted truth. If they believe it for too long they will begin to harbor bitter feelings towards you. For example, a friend of mine had his wife finally tell him amidst plenty of tears that she felt like she was the sole party responsible for supporting their household. She had "done the math" and he was only working 20-30 hours a week while she continually worked overtime. He would spend his free goofing off, while she was working her butt off.

The friend knew this was not true. He'd been working overtime as well for the past 6 months. So, without getting angry, he showed her his paystubs for the past 6 months proving that he too was working overtime. Then he started listing off all of the odd jobs he had gotten the past 6 months to earn extra money in the meantime.

His wife quickly realized that she had been believing a perception because he did tend to get off earlier than her, and they were able to smooth things over from there.

Think what would have happened had he exploded then and there and told her just how wrong, stupid, and ungrateful she was before storming off. Things would not have gone well, and the problem would have been allowed to compound itself for even longer. When little things like this pop up, you need to nip it in the bud before it is allowed to grow the fruit of something worse.

Proverbs 17:14 – "The beginning of strife is like releasing water; therefore stop contention before a quarrel starts."

I'll end with this, ya'll, because I think it sums up what love is all about and will help you to keep in mind just what is necessary to ensure that a relationship is strong, healthy, and filled with a feeling of being at home.

Love suffers long and is kind; love does not envy; love does not parade itself, is not puffed up; does not behave rudely, does not seek its own, is not provoked, thinks no evil; does not rejoice in iniquity, but rejoices in the truth; bears all things, believes all things, hopes all things, endures all things. Love never fails.

1 Corinthians 13:4-8a

Choose Your Battles

Welcome to a relationship, where you can single-handedly ruin everyone's day by getting into an argument over which side of the cabinet the cups should be placed on. If you think I'm making this stuff up, just wait. There are much stupider reasons out there than that which couples get in fights over. Seriously, it's almost as bad as 5 siblings.

There are some things that you're just not gonna like. If it were 100% up to *you* (and it's not), then you would do things differently. You've got to learn what things are actually worth arguing over, and which things are not. The big stuff such as when to have kids, was your spouse rude to a family member, where to live, and so on are things that may be worth having a disagreement over. The little stuff rarely is.

This principle even extends to small darts that get thrown your way verbally. Oftentimes we'll be insulted by something that may seem incredibly small to the other person. You don't want to be a doormat, nor let your significant other be constantly insensitive, but you also don't have to explode at every minor insult, whether perceived or reality.

What helps me get through these is a verse in Proverbs that says, "It is to a wise man's glory to overlook an insult." Yeah, there are things that I need to respond to. But there are a whole lot of other ones that I can overlook for the greater good of the relationship and happiness of others.

How to Plan a Wedding

I like to kid my wife that I could plan a wedding in a day. She says there's no way and that I don't understand what's all involved, but I still sincerely believe I could get it done in at least a week. Ask any guy. They'll tell you the same thing.

There are plenty of great resources out there to help you with planning this special day if you've finally reached that stage in your life, but here is a very, very scaled-down checklist of some of the things that you're going to have to start researching.

The wife is going to be the one who is going to do the majority of the planning. In my experience, and from watching the interactions of other couples through this phase, it's best if the dude takes a back seat. Otherwise, all he does is add extra stress. She's the one that's been dreaming of this day her entire life. Guys have been dreaming of the wedding night.

So, let them plan all that mess and the guys should focus on having the honeymoon and living arrangements all taken care of in detail so that she doesn't have anything to worry about at all from those two things.

Girls

- Book a venue

- Book a photographer (you get what you pay for here!)
- Catering
- Reception site chosen
- Guest list
- Bridesmaids Chosen
- Bridesmaids Dresses
- Groomsmen Tuxes
- Invitations/Who's Invited?
- Flowers
- Wedding Bands
- Decorations
- Pastor chosen

Guys

- Groomsmen Chosen
- Honeymoon location chosen
- Honeymoon hotel booked
- Honeymoon transportation taken care of
- Honeymoon activities organized
- Post-honeymoon housing set up

Yeah, once again I realize that this is a very simplistic list and some of you girls are probably laughing at my ignorance right about now, but this is just to get you thinking so that the ball gets rolling. Truthfully, this is more for the men than it is for the girls. The girls probably have everything figured out already. The guys are the ones who are most likely to be absolutely clueless about where to start.

How to Get a Passport

Whether you're studying abroad or finally are going on that trip to Italy you've always dreamed about, if you leave the US you are going to have to get a passport. In my experience this is an absolute pain in the butt of a process, but here are the tips that will help it go as smoothly as possible for you.

Start looking up the paperwork and stuff that you will need early!

Passports can often take up to 3 months to arrive in the mail, and if you wait till the last minute you may not have it in time.

You know what that means? You're not leaving the country.

Call your local post office to schedule a passport appointment.

The post office is where you have to go to get these things done. They're gonna give you some papers to fill out, ask you some questions, and take your picture as well. Be aware that most post offices tend to operate on a skeleton roster and so it may take some time to actually be able to get an appointment.

My post office in the past actually hasn't had somebody there to take pictures of you, something that you need if you want to travel. It can't just be any picture either. It has to be a particular size with a particular background. Walmart often has a photographer on staff that can get these pictures taken for you pretty cheaply and conveniently.

Expect to pay a good chunk of change.

I believe my first passport cost me around $150. It's not something you can do if you're flat broke.

For more information on this one, I highly recommend going straight to the source at the USPS. They'll be able to tell you exactly what you need, where the closest application center near you is, and when they have available appointment slots. Visit https://www.usps.com/international/passports.htm for more info.

How to Tie a Tie

As much as it pains me to say it, sometimes you just have to wear a tie. Whether it be an interview, funeral, wedding, or for your job knowing how to ensure you are slowly suffocating throughout the day is a useful skill.

There are multiple ways to tie a tie but I've found learning the half-Windsor knot to be one of the quickest knots to learn, and it looks halfway decent as well.

1. Drape the tie around your neck, and adjust it so that the small end is hanging right above your belly button. The small end of the tie is essentially going to remain stationary throughout the entire tying process. Only move the thick end. For the sake of clarity, keep the small end of the tie on your left side.
2. Move the wide end over the top of the small end.
3. Wrap the wide end underneath of the small end and then bring the wide end back to your right side.
4. Now bring the wide end up towards your face.
5. Pass the wide end underneath the newly formed "collar" of the tie and bring it towards your left side.
6. Bring the wide end now across the front of the small end towards your right side.
7. Now bring the wide end up underneath of the collar and straight up to the top of your head.
8. There will be a triangle-shaped knot forming right at the nape of your neck. You need to now take the

wide end of the tie and pull it underneath the horizontal piece of tie that is in the front of that triangle-shaped knot.
9. Pull the wide end all the way down towards your waist, and then pull the small end of the tie to adjust it. Voila. You've tied a half-Windsor.
10. Ideally, the wide end of the tie should just barely touch your belt line. If it ends halfway up your chest you look like an idiot. If it ends down by your crotch, you look like a slob. If it takes multiple tries, that's fine, just do what you can to get the tie as close to the top of the beltline as possible.

How to Vote

Nothing spices up Facebook and Twitter like election season. There's just nothing like discovering your cousins in another state think that everyone who is voting for your candidate is wicked and potentially worth imprisonment. Talk about an interesting Thanksgiving dinner.

Anyways, you live in America. We are the land of the free, and with that freedom comes the responsibility to vote for who you believe would be the best choice for the office that is up for grabs. If you don't vote, do you really have a right to complain about what is happening in your country? I don't think so. So in order to let your voice be heard, here is what you need to do.

Research the candidates.

Look online and find out what each candidate stands for. You don't want to just blindly vote for a candidate because they're hotter, better dressed, or your friends are voting for them. Doing so may cause you to be endorsing something that you find absolutely disgusting.

Do your research to get a better idea of their platform, and only then should you make your decision.

Fill out a voter registration form online.

This little form means that you are legally allowed to vote. You are a citizen of the United States, and you want to have a stick in the fire of this election. Make sure that you are registered to vote or you may end up disappointed with your inability to do so when you finally get to the booth.

Many states have a deadline to register as well. In my state, you have to register something like 4 weeks prior to the actual election. The registration deadline isn't advertised or anything like that. They just expect you to know it. And if you miss it, you're screwed and the registration office will act like you're an ignorant moron.

Don't go through that headache.

Look this up as soon as possible so that you don't miss the deadline for your state.

After a few days of filling this form out, you should get your voter registration card in the mail. Keep this in a secure place, and bring it with you when you show up to vote.

Hit the polls.

You need to know what date the election is, and where you are supposed to go to vote as well. The county that you live in is going to be divided into different sections called 'precincts'. A precinct determines where everybody in that area is supposed to vote. On two separate occasions, I've shown up to vote at the wrong voting booth on Election Day and been turned away. You need to make sure that you are voting where you have been told you must vote.

You also need to ensure that you are bringing your ID with you to this one. Your voter registration card and your driver's license should suffice on proving that you are who you really say you are.

Where to Buy Stamps

You can buy stamps at your local post office. The teller can always sell them to you, but I've also noticed that many post offices out where I live are now installing stamp dispensers. You walk up, punch in what you want, swipe your credit card, and stamps are dispensed. I prefer face to face contact, but whatever.

If you'd rather print stamps out from the comfort of your own home you could always print them out on stamps.com. You're still gonna have to pay for them that way, but it may save you a trip to the post office. Stamps.com I really don't recommend unless you do a lot of shipping and mailing. It operates on a subscription basis which may actually cost you more than it's worth if you're just mailing out the occasional crop of monthly bills.

Currently, stamps cost 60 cents each. Going to the post office and paying for one stamp at a time is a pain, so instead when I swing by there every once in a while I buy a "book" or two of stamps. The books I have are really just small strips of paper with stamps stuck to them, but they contain 20 stamps each. You can buy stamps in rolls as well if you need a whole lot of them, but no matter which way you swing it a stamp is going to cost you 49 cents.

The type of stamp that you're going to want for regular

bills and letters is going to be a "Forever" stamp. These can have all kinds of different designs on them, from Batman to Abe Lincoln to Picasso, but they all say the word 'forever' on them somewhere.

When mailing letters, one 'forever' stamp will ship 1 oz. That typically is around 4-5 pages. If you try to ship anything heavier than that with one 'forever' stamp it will be returned to you with a message saying that there was not enough postage attached. If you have suspicions as to whether a letter is too heavy, weigh it. If you don't have a scale that handles ounces, the cashier at the post office will tell you if you need additional postage.

Mailing Things Bigger than Letters

Let's say it's your nephew's 5th birthday but he lives 13 hours away. He's huge into Spiderman, and you found him an incredible Spiderman action figure that you think he'll love. How do you get it to him?

Get a cardboard box big enough to fit the item.

The post office will sell these, but you'll probably find a better price at Walmart.

Pack the item inside with appropriate stuffing to keep the item from being damaged inside the box during shipping.

If it's a fragile item, use packing peanuts and/or bubble wrap. You can typically get these at Walmart or the UPS store. If it's not so fragile, I like to crumble up pieces of the newspaper or magazine pages and throw them in there.

Tape the box closed with *packing tape*.

Do not use regular scotch tape here. *It will not hold.* You can get packing tape pretty cheap at Walmart. Get your own packing tape too. Don't expect the shipper to do it for you without a price.

Address it.

Write the address of who you are shipping the package to on a side of the box around the middle of that particular face.

Add your return address.

Write your address or the address you would like the package to be returned to should they not be able to deliver the package to who you're sending it to in the top left corner of the same side of the box that you wrote the other address on.

Take the box to the post office, UPS store, or FedEx store and pay to ship it.

Please don't just stick it in your mailbox with a bunch of stamps on it. That's how you get made fun of in the mailman breakroom.

When it comes to shipping packages, you should know that the bigger the box is, the more you are going to pay to ship. Likewise, the heavier the box is, the more you are going to pay to ship. Always do what you can to keep the size of the box as small as possible while still allowing for adequate packing material around the actual item inside.

The farther away that you have to ship an item, the more you are going to pay as well. If you live in Florida, you're going to pay a lot more to ship something to Oregon than you are to ship something to Georgia. So keep all that in mind.

If you do the math and the price just seems way too

pricey, try looking at the post office's Flat Rate Priority Mail boxes. They'll be in the lobby, but basically, it's just a box that you can take that costs one flat rate regardless of where it's going or the weight (to an extent. You probably won't be shipping dumbbells for a flat rate.)

This can be pretty sweet if you can ship an item for $7.00 that was going to cost you $15 or more prior, so check it out. It may be worth your time.

Here's a little-known secret as well. If you're shipping a book to somebody, you can use what's called 'media mail' at the post office. Shipping media mail can drastically lower the price of what you're shipping. Just make sure you don't attempt shipping other items via media mail. They X-ray these and will hit you with a fine if they catch you trying to buck the system.

JOB

You are likely to spend more of your waking hours at your job than you will anywhere else. It's important to do what you can to ensure this isn't as miserable of an existence as possible with your job. Part of that comes from attitude. Part of that comes from finding a job that meshes with how you are wired.

Let's take a look at what that entails...

How to Choose a Job You'd Be Happy With

Man, this is a big one. Who hasn't had the 20-something-year-old existential crisis of trying to figure out what you are supposed to be? I've had a few of them, and there are some lessons that I have learned from them that may help you out. These aren't written for the person who feels a specific calling to go into a certain field. If you know you have a calling to do something, then you can remain pretty confident in what decisions you need to make.

The following advice is for the person that doesn't exactly feel a specific calling. They know they want to be able to support themselves, they want to make a difference, they want to pay off bills, but they also want to be happy with what they do, and with so many choices they are paralyzed with indecision.

If *that* describes you, then keep reading below to see if any of this helps:

What are your skills?

The first thing that I tell people to do is to take an honest look at what they are good at. If you're good with numbers, good at working with tools, great with talking with anybody about anything, or an excellent salesman, then that may help to give you something of an idea of what you should pursue.

Ben Carson wrote an excellent book titled *Think Big* where he talks about his decision to become a brain surgeon. He knew that he was called to be a doctor, but he didn't know exactly what type. He did a ton of praying, but he also took a solid look at his gifts (you have gifts too, in case you didn't know). He knew that he was great at thinking through 3D objects abstractly and had a steady hand, and so recognizing those two traits guided him to being a brain surgeon.

What are your gifts?

If you really don't know what your gifts are, ask your parents or a close friend. It's funny how we're often oblivious toward the obvious in our own lives.

What makes you happy?

Nobody wants to be miserable. I've worked several jobs that put bread on the table (albeit that was about it), yet that made me absolutely miserable. I worked for a particular clothing brand's distribution center and it was almost as if they tried to make you angry/sad/apathetic/unhappy.

If you're making a ton of money doing what you're doing, but honestly dread getting out of bed every morning to do what you do, maybe it's time to look at something else. My dad has always said that the money is important, but it should come second. Find what you truly enjoy, and learn to live within the means that that job gives you.

Yeah, you may not be able to take the fantastic overseas vacations every year that your friends are, but if you are having an absolute ball at work every day providing for yourself and your family, does that really matter?

Don't be afraid to experiment.

Oftentimes people find out that they like a job that they never would have guessed would have played to their likes, strengths, and abilities. Try new things. Learn as much as you can. I know a number of friends who have done really well, and genuinely enjoy what they do but they never originally set out with the intent of being a manager at so-and-so

Remember you can always change it.

Even if you do make a mistake, or discover that the job you got isn't the one you want, you can always change careers. This isn't something that you end up locked into for life. Sure you don't want to waste several hundred thousand dollars on medical school to find out you hate it (I have a friend that did that), but it is possible to change careers without wasting hard-earned money and precious time.

If you really want further advice on the subject, I highly recommend *What Color is Your Parachute?* I've read through different editions of it several times over the past decade or so, and there's a reason that it's a national bestseller. It is hands down one of the best books out there on helping people to discover what their gifts are and what makes them happy. When you know these two things, you are able to narrow down your job choices drastically, and it can greatly reduce the stress of looking for jobs.

For even further reading on the subject, I found Ben Carson's book *Think Big: Unleashing Your Potential for Excellence* to be very beneficial as well. He goes into much further detail about how to know not only what your gifts are but helps you to discover what would be a good fit for you as well.

How to Look for a Job

I'm going to give it to you straight: looking for a job is going to be one of the most stressful things that you'll do immediately after college/high school. For some reason, employers have now decided that they want to know your entire life history, your greatest phobia, and what the name of your firstborn will be. Not really, but I'm trying to make a point. Applications are ridiculous.

Add to that the fact that most job applications are going to take you 45 minutes to an hour for the chance to *maybe* get an interview, and you'll understand why looking for a job can be so stressful. It's no fun to spend hour after hour working for free.

Nevertheless, if you want to eat non-dumpster food you need to finish an application. However, you also need to know where to look for jobs that you would like in the first place that will allow you to not only pay your bills, but pay off your student loans, and save for the future.

I have literally filled out hundreds of job applications over the years, so I feel like I'm getting pretty proficient at this. Here are the five main places where I look for jobs:

Indeed.com

This is hands down the best job site out there. You will be able to find essentially every job that's posted via indeed.com. It's incredibly user-friendly, it saves your recent searches, and it will send you notifications whenever there is a job posted that sounds similar to something that you would be interested in. When starting your job search, I highly recommend turning to indeed.com first.

Monster.com

Though not as comprehensive as indeed.com, I have found some very good job opportunities posted here that weren't posted elsewhere for whatever reason. It's not that this site isn't a good resource, it's just not as popular as indeed, and for that reason, I tend to stick with it as a backup.

Your state's .gov page

If what you want to do is something where you would have to work for the government, your state's .gov page (e.g. Virginia.gov) may contain a large number of potential job opportunities that may not be posted elsewhere. I've found state professor gigs, police officer postings, public health work, and government office positions posted here very frequently. Check it out. You may be pleasantly surprised by what you find.

Asking managers of places you'd be interested in

A lot of smaller mom-and-pop-type stores may not have jobs posted online. As a result, the only way you would ever know if they need extra help is if you go into them looking presentable and ask. Be professional when you do this. First impressions are everything here, and this isn't the time to come in looking like a slob or being curt with your speech. I've done this with farm work before by going into my local Southern States and asking if they knew of any shepherds who needed part-time help. Southern States didn't have any positions, but they put me in contact with somebody who did.

Word of mouth

If your friends and family know that you are looking for a job in a particular field, they will act as 'feelers' in the community for you. When a potential position gets mentioned in conversation, they will have you in mind and be able to put you in contact with who you need to talk with. For example, a friend of mine knew I was looking for online professor work. She was currently one, and when her boss mentioned that they needed an extra editor for an online anatomy course that they were creating, she immediately gave him my info. Let your friends know what you are looking for, and repay them with a cup of coffee to say thanks after you land the position.

Sell yourself

Before you think I'm suggesting getting engaged in prostitution hear me out. It is possible to create a job for yourself just by "selling" or pitching your talents and abilities to somebody. I've done this with shepherds in my area. I'm really interested in working with sheep and goats. I went to the local farm store and saw an ad from a local farmer advertising sheep for sale. I called them up and told them who I was, what I could do, and asked if they needed any part-time help. I now help them clean stalls and shear sheep occasionally.

That job didn't exist at all before. It wasn't on any site, they didn't even advertise needing any help. But I was able to sell myself and create the position. This is possible in more areas than you think. It just takes a bit of creativity, visible enthusiasm/confidence, and some initiative. Don't be afraid to think outside of the box with this one.

So let's say you finally find a job that you would be interested in, or you find a number of them that you would be interested in. What do you do then? Prepare for the long haul, because you're in for a load of work, but I have found that there is one helpful tip that can save you a ton of time after your first application.

As you're going through your first application, keep note of what questions they are asking you. Most likely they're going to want to know your education history, your contact info, and your job history for x amount of years. They may also ask for a resume and cover letter as well.

I've found that keeping a Word document with all of that info already on it saves me a lot of time from having to re-research everything with every new application. I don't remember my GPA from high school or college off the top of my head. I don't remember the exact date range I've worked for every company in the past, nor my manager's phone numbers off the top of my head either.

However, by keeping all of this information in a Word

document already pre-typed I can simply refer to it while I am filling out each application in the future instead of having to dig through all of my old files over and over again.

Your resume is going to remain pretty static, so I just make small changes to it as time goes on (new jobs, education, etc.) and submit the same one to every employer. I do the exact same thing with a cover letter as well. I have a pretty generic one that I've typed up that I'll slightly modify for each new position that I'm applying for. I'll change the name of who the cover letter is addressed to real quick, and then add 2-3 sentences that make it sound like I specifically wrote the letter for that company.

It saves me a ton of time, and I'm able to submit quality work in a reasonable amount of time.

How to Write a Resume

I've been involved in the hiring process a bit at some of the different places that I've worked, and I've had to write my resume a number of times as well. Writing a resume isn't as daunting of a task as you may have been led to believe. What it all boils down to is making yourself look as good as possible to your potential employer. You definitely don't want to lie or anything like that ("yeah, Mars was pretty nice"), but you do want to make hiring you look like a wise decision on the employer's part.

Here's what I do for mine, and what I look for in prospects' resumes.

Your name, email address, phone number, and address should go in the top left corner. I want to know whose resume I am reading and the best way to get into contact with them, and I want that information to be as easy to find as possible. Knowing that humanity is inherently lazy, do you really want to make your employer have to *search* for your contact info should your resume show promise? No. No, you don't.

Make that stuff easy to find.

I place job experience underneath that. I don't place every job I've ever done, but I do place the past 3-5 of them anyway. I use bullet points for each job, put a time-frame for each position, and then give a very brief description of what I used to do there.

Underneath my work history, I list my education history. Here I list grad school, college, high school, and whatever other education you may have all in chronological order. Let them know what your major was at these schools as well as if you had any special distinctions while there (e.g. valedictorian).

Next, I list community involvement or certifications. You could potentially list both if you wanted to, but that's up to you. For community involvement, I list all of the random things that I have done for the community in the past that I think may help the employer to think that I am a good hire. For certifications, spell out what you have, who you got it through, and potentially your score as well if it's really good.

Lastly, I list my references. I try to put three on there with their full names, phone numbers, email addresses, where they work, what they do, and how I know them (e.g. previous boss/coworker/etc.)

Try to get all of this to fit on one page if you can, and don't use any stupid-looking font. You want the whole thing to look classy. If you follow all of the above recommendations, you'll have a very good resume that will help you in your job search.

Basic Interview Skills

So, you finally got the interview, huh? That's great! I've interviewed several people, and here is what I've noticed are some of the trends with the best interviews we've had.

Dress up and dress professionally.

I always find it awkward at interviews when you can tell the person didn't even try to look nice. In many cases, this interview is going to be your first impression. First impressions are incredibly important, so make sure that you get them right. You may not get the job otherwise.

Do I like dressing up? Nope. I absolutely hate it. But if you are going to an interview you have to. Guys, you need to wear dress pants or khakis (NOT SHORTS!), a dress shirt that's tucked in, dress shoes, and a belt. Make sure your clothes are ironed, your hair is presentable, your facial hair isn't hobo-ish, and that your breath doesn't smell like dog doo-doo. You may want to consider a suit or tie as well depending on what you are applying for.

Ladies, you don't have as many rules on this one. You just need to ensure that you're dressed nicely. However, you also need to make sure that you're not coming across as sleazy, aka keep your boobs in your shirt. I've seen a number of women who don't seem to understand the last part. They'll arrive at work with dress clothes, but the shirt is low enough to get them a plethora of free drinks at the bar.

Don't do that. Be professional.

Research the company beforehand.

It's always a pleasant surprise when an interviewee is able to ask me a meaningful question about the company that relates to the job they are applying for. That tells they did their research. I think it also shows initiative, and as a result, it scores points.

Ask questions.

Asking questions shows that you have given working at that particular company a degree of thought. Ask questions about what a typical day looks like,

Relax.

Feel stressed out and uptight? Yeah, we can tell. Don't be afraid of the interviewers. Just relax and be at ease. They're normal people just like you. Yes, you want to take your interview seriously, it's not something to treat as trivial, but you also want to show the employer that you can handle uncomfortable situations without making everybody else feel uncomfortable too.

Pretend it's just a casual conversation you're having on the street with just some random stranger, and go from there. Just make sure to sprinkle in your "Yes, sirs" and "Yes, ma'ams".

Show up early.

Being late for an interview doesn't bode well.

Basic Job Skills

I train a lot of interns where I work. I've also been involved in the hiring process for a good number of our employees. That being said, I'm constantly surprised at the lack of just basic job skills by a lot of the people that come looking to us for employment.

Some of this may come across as common knowledge, but if you really want to not only exceed at your job but be likely to get that promotion, here's what you need to do.

Constantly look for work to do while at work.

When management asks me if we should hire a particular intern or not, I always think back to their work ethic first. Were they taking initiative? If the answer is no, then my answer is no. That company has enough lazy people working for it already, functioning as nothing more than useless parasites to the business as they relax during their "down time" at work.

You're at work. There is no "downtime". Find something to do, even if it seems that there's nothing to do. Clean, send out emails, do some marketing – just do *something*. Your employer will notice. I promise you.

Don't talk politics while on the clock.

You're passionate about politics? Cool. Me too. But being

on the clock is not the time to voice your current opinion on the latest election results. Here's what'll end up happening. You'll either piss off a customer, piss off a fellow employee, or piss off somebody from upper management.

If you make a customer mad, they may never come back, may leave a negative review about the business online, may tell their friends not to shop there, or may complain to your manager. Not a single one of these outcomes is good, and every single one of them will result in your manager being mad at you.

If you make a fellow employee mad you may be surprised to discover just how quickly a friend can turn into a viper. I personally experienced this and it almost cost me my job. I have had friends almost lose their jobs because of voicing their opinions or for telling jokes that other employees then used as ammunition against them. I don't believe you need to walk on eggshells around the workplace, but do practice discretion with what you say and around who.

If you tick off a manager with your political view, I'll let your imagination run wild with what the results of that one could be. Humans are humans. And if someone has a perception of the kind of person you are because of your political beliefs it could cost you the promotion or job that you've been after.

There's nothing wrong with having opinions. You have freedom of speech. But when you are on the clock you are representing the company that you work for and you do not want to bite the hand that feeds you without good reason.

Stay off your cellphone while on the clock.

Cellphones make you look like you really don't care about your job. And maybe that is the case. But you need to give the appearance that you do at least if you don't want to be the first person the boss marks off the list when downsizing comes.

If you make a mistake, own up to it.

If you screw up (and you will), just admit it, apologize, fix it, learn from it, and do better next time. People respect you when you do that. It's when you attempt to hide it or pass off the blame to somebody else that you end up really showing the low quality of a person you are.

Communicate.

The failure to communicate ends up just creating headaches. Make sure that you communicate everything you need to with everybody that you need to.

Don't show up late.

Be early. Bosses know who is consistently late and who is not, and they do not forget easily.

If a customer needs you to show them something, show them.

Don't just point in the general direction and walk away. Holy smokes it makes me mad when employees do this.

No attitude.

You can have a rough day inside, but don't let that show to the customers or employees around you. If they are the cause, use your discretion and ability to communicate to fix the problem, but in no circumstance should you let your problems at home or whatever impact the way that you treat your customers. Swallow that and deal with it when you're not on the clock.

Watch what you say.

Aside from political stuff, you need to be careful about the complaints you make within your company as well. People backstab and sabotage incredibly quickly. I've listened in on numerous conversations with coworkers who have done so to other coworkers. Just 2 minutes prior both people were in the same room and you would have thought they were the best of friends. As soon as that other person leaves the room though something changes, and I'm not sure what.

So, just be mindful of what you say and to whom. If you have a legitimate complaint, not some childish problem caused by your oversensitivity with another coworker, then take it up the ladder to your *immediate* supervisor. Don't bypass them unless you absolutely have to, and don't complain to the people that are under your management. Complaints should almost always go one rung up and stop there.

How to Open a Business

If you're entrepreneurially minded you may want to open up your own business. I think that's great. Historically, owning a business is one of the best ways to make money. There are a couple of legal hoops to jump through if you want to start one though. Because there are so many different types of business, each requiring different paperwork, licenses, insurance, etc. we'll just stick to the absolute bare bones here.

The first thing that you're going to need to do is to apply for a business license at your local city hall. They will most likely make you go to the courtroom to apply for a name for your business after you search through gigantic, dusty old books containing the names of every business ever ran in your particular town. Once you've found an unused name, you fill out the paperwork, take it back to the proper person and they'll walk you through it from there.

You're going to have to choose what type of business license you want. The three main business license types are sole proprietorship, joint venture, and a limited liability company.

A sole proprietorship is going to be the easiest business license to get (read: there's less paperwork). This business license basically says that you personally run the company and that you personally are responsible for it. This is good in the sense that you didn't have a bunch of hoops to jump through, but can be bad if something bad happens and somebody sues your business. Because with a sole proprietorship somebody doesn't just sue your business, they sue *you*. This means that *all* of your personal belongings could potentially be taken away from you, even your car, home, and life savings provided you get sued.

Now some businesses are going to be more at risk for this than others. If you're in the health industry such as personal training, the food industry, or something similar where there is a chance that people could get hurt using your services, eating your food, or using your product (such as if you're a gunsmith or you built a deck wrong) then it may be a good idea to stay away from getting a sole proprietorship.

You can often find relatively cheap insurance for whatever field that you are in to cover your losses up to a certain extent if you get sued, but if there's any chance that those medical bills from the person you hurt could exceed that then you may be best off getting something else.

A limited liability company, or LLC, is a safer way to conduct business in my opinion. There is a lot more paperwork to go through, and it is a bit more mysterious to find out what paperwork you actually need to sign, but it can be done. However, once you have the LLC in your name nobody can personally sue you for harm that was done through your business.

That means if somebody slips on the floor at your coffee shop and breaks their tail bone, requiring emergency surgery, months of physical therapy, months of prescription painkillers, months of missed work, and pain and suffering payment that they can only get money from your business.

Once the business runs out of money, that person cannot come to you looking for you to pay the difference from your personal funds.

SCHOOL

Hand-in-hand with finding a job that you enjoy is finding a school that will help you to qualify for that job. While I personally feel that post-high school educations are overrated, there are some positions that you'll never get without that degree in hand.

It's important to know a thing or two about school as a result. Here's what school should have taught you about itself.

Looking at Continuing Your Education

So you're thinking about going back to school, huh? Well, that can be a noble goal. It can also be a major decision. If you know that you want a particular job, let's say you want to be a lawyer or your boss wants you to have a college education in order for you to get promoted, then yes, you're going to have to go back to school.

There are a number of factors that you're going to have to consider though when choosing whether to re-enroll in class again or not.

Is it a sound investment?

Please don't just go back to school hoping that it will 'open up new doors' for you. I don't believe that in today's society that is the case. (Some of my family will disagree with me on this one, but I still think I'm right.)

Go to school with a target in mind. Know the end goal beforehand. If you just go to experiment and see what it is that you like, you're going to end up on the backside of that degree with a lot of unnecessary debt that can really impact your life for decades. Student loans are no joke, and you can't just declare bankruptcy and get out of them. Student loans stick around with you regardless of whether you go bankrupt or not.

So before you spend tens of thousands of dollars on schooling, ask yourself if it is really worth it. Will that degree pay off? Will it offer you a chance at the job you really want, and will the paycheck be worth how much you put into the degree? If you're majoring in English, history, psychology, women's studies, or music I would argue rather vehemently that it won't.

Don't go to college or grad school just for the heck of it. View it as a financial investment that should pay big dividends in the future. If you knew there was a mutual fund you could invest in that was going to tank later on costing you years of work, tens of thousands of dollars, and emotional strain would you invest in it? Nope. View school as the same way. If the return isn't worth it, why would you do it?

How will you pay for it?

Most high school students that I've met aren't too concerned with this. Four years is an awful long time away. They can worry about the money then, right? Wrong.

You have to have a game plan. If school is not economically feasible, please don't just take out student loans for the whole thing and pay the sticker price. There are plenty of scholarships and grants out there that can help you here. Your employer may even cover some of the cost. The hospital where my wife works pays up to $4000/year for nurses who want to further their education. Where you work may have a similar deal. It's worth looking into and taking advantage of if you can.

Look at the price of classes where you're interested in as well. Shop around at different colleges. You'll find drastic differences in pricing. Just choosing the cheaper college could easily save you $10,000 or more.

Are you willing to change your lifestyle?

There were many many times during school when my friends went out and had fun while I sat behind a computer analyzing chemistry equations or whatnot. I missed a lot of birthdays. I stayed indoors on many a beautiful Saturday. When friends went out at night, I often stayed at the library finishing yet another paper.

That is what school is like. It does require some sacrifices to be made if you want to get through it with your GPA in one piece, which you do by the way. Why pay for a degree when you don't act as if it is worth it? Why put years of your life into something, only to do a shoddy job, and then have future potential employers view you as a shoddy potential employee?

If you go to school things are going to change. I can remember this being one of the key reasons that I didn't go to medical school. I was seriously considering it for a while. I had scoped out the schools, had a good idea of pricing, was ready to move, was prepping for the MCAT, had the prerequisite courses mostly taken care of from my undergraduate degree, and everything.

Eventually, I was able to talk with the dean of one of the medical schools I was interested in. I asked him what I could expect with the workload. I didn't have any fantasies that medical school was going to be easy, but I wanted to know what his experiences were. He said that he studied, went to class, did rotations, and did lab work 70-80 hours/week while he was in school. When I asked if he had time to do anything fun he responded that he could play basketball for an hour every Tuesday night if he managed his time right.

Right then and there I knew that medical school wasn't for me. Only having fun for an hour a week for 7+ years? Yeah, no thanks.

The point is though that you have to be prepared to change how you currently live if you want to get that degree.

How to Apply to College

Let's say that you've finally decided that for you college is the next step. That's a big decision. Not to add to the pressure that you're already going to be facing at this moment in your life, but the decision to go to college is not something to be taken lightly.

Why?

It's expensive and takes up a lot of time (usually 4 years for a bachelor's degree). So if you've made it through that entire fretting stage and are confident that college is what you want to do to get to the career that you want to do, then there are a series of steps that you are going to need to make to get started applying.

Take the SAT or ACT exam.

Colleges require that you take one of these two exams to be qualified to get into college. Even if your score is poor you may still get into a college, but the higher you score on these exams, the better are your chances are of actually getting into the college that you would like.

Take these exams seriously. Aside from the higher score meaning an increased chance of actually getting into college, the higher your score on these the more scholarship money you'll be able to win for college. That extra $1000 per semester may not seem like much now, but that money quickly adds up, and with a four-year degree, that $1000/semester scholarship will have saved you $8000. It takes a long time to pay back 8 grand.

There are a number of resources out there to help you to prepare to take one of these. I personally signed up for a 6 AM prep class every morning for two weeks for the SAT. It was expensive, but it gave me a better idea of what to expect. I also checked out numerous SAT workbooks from the library and made it a point to work my way through a bit of them for about an hour or two each night.

You don't have to take both exams, only one. They are both very different from one another. I actually scored lower on my SAT than I would have liked. So I took the ACT afterward. I didn't need to, but the score that I got on the ACT actually qualified me for scholarship money that I wouldn't have gotten otherwise with my SAT score. So do what you can here and strategize a bit with your options.

Look at the 'Admission' or 'Prospective Students' pages on your colleges of choice's websites.

There are going to be a number of different pieces of paperwork that different colleges require. One of the key things that you need to look for right now is when the application deadline is. You want to have everything turned in by that point or you can say bye-bye to attending college there next semester. Colleges don't make exceptions here. Do the paperwork and get it turned in on time.

What is this paperwork? Well, it varies from place to place. Most colleges require an educational resume of sorts listing your grades, extracurricular activities, and other academic accomplishments. Even non-school stuff can be included in this. For example, I have a friend who ended up getting into UVA, an incredibly difficult school to get into. He was smart, but there were a lot of other applicants with better grades than his who were applying.

What does he believe helped to set him apart? He had been to China numerous times to teach English. How many other people do you know that have done that? The extra stuff helps, so include it too.

Another piece of paperwork that you're going to probably have to submit is an application essay that generally asks you to briefly describe who you are and why they should let you into their college. I'd recommend getting your high school English teacher or somebody else you know who's good at editing to look over this one for you after you type it up. You do want to make sure that this is something that looks good. Sloppiness on this essay doesn't make you look like a good candidate.

The only exception to this I would say is if you are reeeeeally good at a sport. If the school has decided that you are going to play on their team, you could essentially think that a rock is a type of vegetable and you're gonna make it in. So if you have the recruiters looking your way, do your best here regardless, but they're gonna walk you through the entire process.

Get your financial paperwork in order.

One of the main things that you're going to want to make sure you have done is to file your FAFSA. A FAFSA is something that qualifies you for student aid (read: free money). You have to make sure that you have this submitted on time. To procrastinate on getting this one in on time is a special kind of stupid because it could literally cost you tens of thousands of dollars.

Yeah, it's a pain in the butt, but I guarantee you that it is well worth it. If you have questions throughout the process call your college's financial aid department. They will know the content inside and out and they can walk you through the entire process. They'll let you know what paperwork you need to file, and will somewhat point the way to what scholarships that you qualify for.

If you're going to a school that is within the state that you are a resident of check to see if you get discounted tuition for that. Many states offer great scholarships for residents of their own state, and once again this can save you thousands of dollars. If you're going to a school that's out of state for you, you're out of luck on this one, but there are literally thousands of other scholarships out there that you may qualify for.

Look for scholarships.

This is one of the most daunting parts of college if you ask me. The scholarship search always stressed me out. Fortunately, there are plenty of sources out there that strive to make it easier for you. This subject is rather lengthy so it's received its own chapter

How to Find Scholarships for College

College is incredibly expensive, and paying the full sticker price of any university is just outright stupid. Thankfully, there is a wide range of scholarships available out there for the taking for which you can qualify for just about any reason you can think of. Yeah, applying for these things does take a lot of work, and can essentially qualify as a hobby, but if you can make $4000 off of 3 hours that you put into an essay for a random scholarship, the time is well worth it. You won't make that at McDonald's.

I spent countless hours researching scholarships while in college, and here is what I have found to be the best resources available.

Cappex.com – This was my favorite way of looking for scholarships online. With Cappex, you have to fill out a rather lengthy profile of yourself but it'll list every scholarship it can find out there that you qualify for. There are literally scholarships out there for any reason you can think of. True, many are for people who write very good essays on particular subjects or are essentially a lottery for people with good grades, but there are others out there that you may qualify for simply because you are left-handed, are a certain race, are 6 feet tall, or like certain types of music.

All you have to do is look. Did I win any scholarships from Cappex? Nope. Though I did apply for dozens of them. However, that doesn't mean that this isn't a great resource to check out to at least get you thinking about some of the options out there for you.

Fastweb.com – This and Cappex are probably the two most widely known college scholarship websites out there. The good thing about this site is that lots of people who want to provide scholarships know about it. The bad thing is that a lot of students know about it as well. Nevertheless, this one is still worth the look if for no other reason than that it gives you ideas of where to look elsewhere in your community for scholarships.

Local scholarships within your community – This is where I feel like you really have a chance to be successful. The downside of online scholarship banks is that literally anybody in the world has the chance to apply for those scholarships. With local scholarships, you can have fantastic odds. Oftentimes local banks, doctor offices, school boards, and who knows what else will offer small scholarships for local potential college students. Though they may be for minuscule amounts compared to what you'll find on Cappex ($500 compared to full-ride scholarships) every little bit counts, and if it only takes you 2 hours to apply for a scholarship that wins you $500, you've made $250/hour. That's pretty good.

Talk with your college's financial aid department – These departments will have books filled with potential scholarships that you may qualify for. It's always worth the effort to spend an hour or so talking with the people here as they will be able to give you advice and steer you towards potential scholarships that you would have had no idea about otherwise.

Don't let all of this overwhelm you. Sure, there's a lot of stuff that seems to come at you at once that you'll be absolutely clueless about once you graduate from high school. The "real" world is a lot different than you probably think. It can be pretty dog-eat-dog.

But don't let it smash you in.

Life is beautiful. It's an amazing ride that you're going to have a lot of fun on. There's gonna be some downs, but there's gonna be a lot of ups as well. You're going to learn a lot. About yourself, about the world, about other people. However, there are a few curve balls that are gonna come your way as well. It's nothing to continually fret about. Worrying quite literally only makes things worse.

However, when some of those curve balls come your way, hopefully, this book will prove its value. Hang on to it. Three years down the road from now you may find yourself face to face with a situation that you were unprepared for, and this book may have the answer.

Once you feel like you've gotten a fairly solid grasp on all of the subjects and scenarios within then give it to somebody else who you love and care for that you want to see given the best preparations they can possibly be given for what all lies before them.

With all that being said, hopefully, by now you've at least been able to glean *something* from this book. It's filled with the lessons that I wish school had taught me instead of pre-calculus and imaginary numbers. Use this info to help others and yourself. I wish you the best of luck.

Sincerely,

Aden Tate

Further Reading

- *The 4-Hour Chef* by Timothy Ferriss
- *What Color is Your Parachute?* by Richard Nelson Bolles
- *The Total Money Makeover* by Dave Ramsey
- *Financial Peace Revisited* by Dave Ramsey
- *Think Big* by Ben Carson
- *Unconditional* by Brian Zahnd
- Proverbs
- *Communicating for a Change* by Andy Stanley and Lane Jones
- *The 5 Love Languages* by Gary Chapman
- *Rich Dad, Poor Dad* by Robert Kiyosaki

References

1. https://ucr.fbi.gov/crime-in-the-u.s/2010/crime-in-the-u.s.-2010/violent-crime/robberymain
2. https://www.aclu.org/know-your-rights/what-do-if-youre-stopped-police-immigration-agents-or-fbi
3. http://www.theblaze.com/news/2014/01/02/here-are-all-the-rights-you-have-when-interacting-with-a-police-officer/
4. https://www.brilliantearth.com/news/a-guys-unbiased-guide-to-engagement-rings/